WHY SO MANY CHURCHES?

D0062581

All scripture references are from the King James Version unless otherwise stated.

WHY SO MANY CHURCHES?
Copyright 1992 by Hearthstone Publishing, Ltd.

Printed in the United States of America

Published by:
Hearthstone Publishing, Ltd.
P.O. Box 815
Oklahoma City, OK 73101
(405) 235-5396 ● 1-800-652-1144 ● FAX (405) 236-4634

ISBN 1-879366-28-2

Table of Contents

Chapter One

Exploring the Differences

In this study on the subject *Why So Many Churches?*, we will attempt to explain the basic reasons why those who are called by the name of Christ are split into hundreds of denominations and sects. Within these multitudinous church organizations, memberships argue over such things as:

- Should communion wine be taken from a single congregational cup or individual cups?
- Should there be instrumental accompaniment to singing?
- Should the church assembly be scheduled for Saturday or Sunday?
- Are the members saved by faith or works or both?
- Is the believer's eternal reward in Heaven or on earth?
- Can a Christian fall from grace and be lost?
- What does church membership have to do with salvation?
- Is Jesus Christ coming back to reign over the earth?
- Is the baptism of the Holy Spirit a second work of grace?
- Do Christians have to speak in unknown tongues?

The previous roster of doctrinal differences contains just a very few of the many areas of controversy which divide Christendom into denominations and sects. I would also point out that these are just the more common differences. There are also major differences such as the divinity of Jesus Christ, His blood atonement, His resurrection from the grave, the infallibility of the Word, supreme authority of Scripture, and the inherent carnality of man.

Investigating the reasons for church differences, I have concluded that they lie in the failure to understand the variance between the gospel of the Kingdom and the gospel of grace; and more specifically, the message preached by Peter and the message preached by Paul. It is my firm conviction that if all churches could agree on the first fifteen chapters of the Acts of the Apostles, there would be few church differences. Therefore, it is important for Christians to understand the difference between the ministry that Christ committed to Peter and the ministry that He committed to Paul. Herein exists the controversy that has resulted in the legion of church divisions, not only in our day, but from the very beginning of the church age.

Some may rightfully ask: "Is there an issue affecting our own personal faith in Christ and the state of salvation involved in this subject of the two gospels?" To this question I answer: As touching the believer's personal faith in Christ and the assurance of his salvation --no; as relating to the general testimony of the church in the world and the evangelizing of the heathen--yes.

To give a personal example, from the beginning of my conversion from a sinner to a child of God through faith in Jesus Christ, I understood and fully believed these essential basic fundamental truths:

1. God through a special creative act made the heavens, the earth, and all things therein.
2. The Bible is the inspired and infallible Word of the

Living God.

3. Adam through transgression fell into sin; and there-after, all men born of Adam are sinners before God: *"For all have sinned, and come short of the glory of God"* (Rom. 3:23).

4. God sent forth His Son, the Lord Jesus Christ (who was conceived by the Holy Spirit and born of a virgin) to redeem sinners from a lost condition and from the condemnation of eternal death in Hell.

5. The Son of God, the Lord Jesus Christ, took our sins upon Himself on the cross and paid the full penalty for our sins. He was judged for our sins in our place.

6. That if a sinner believes this according to John 3:16 and Romans 10:8-10, and turns to Christ by faith according to Ephesians 2:8-9, he is redeemed from his sins, and the Holy Spirit creates in the new believer in Christ a new creation.

7. To all who have been saved by faith in Christ, God has given the promise of eternal life and a glorified body like unto the body of Jesus Christ at the resurrection.

8. Today Christ our Lord and Savior is seated at the right hand of God, just as He arose from the grave after His crucifixion, and He is coming back to this earth to rule as King of kings and Lord of lords at the end of this age of grace.

My belief in these and many other fundamental precepts of God's Word have not changed since the day that I accepted Jesus Christ as my personal Savior. However, the greatest revelation to me concerning dispensational truths and sound doctrine was the scrip-tural evidence that Paul and Peter did not preach the same message. They preached the same Christ, but not the same gospel. I arrived at this conclusion many years after my conversion. I do not claim any special credit for this understanding, for I was helped in arriving at a knowledge of the basic variances between the ministries of Paul and Peter by Bible scholars who had more insight into the Scriptures than I.

In his footnotes to the Bible, Dr. C.I. Scofield outlined many of the differences that existed between the ministries of Paul and Peter. For example, on page 1209 of *The New Scofield Reference Bible*, he writes:

> "...*It is in the Epistles* [of Paul] *that the order, position, privileges, and duties of the church are most fully given....They develop the doctrine of the church....Through Paul was given the detailed revelation of the body of Christ in its heavenly calling, promise, and destiny. The doctrine of grace found in the teaching of Christ is also given further revelation through Paul....*"

In reviewing the ministry of Peter in relation to what Dr. Scofield said about the ministry of Paul, we remember that the authority for Peter's ministry is revealed in Matthew 16:19: *"And I will give unto thee the keys of the kingdom of heaven: and whatsoever thou shalt bind on earth shall be bound in heaven: and whatsoever thou shalt loose on earth shall be loosed in heaven."* If the keys of the Kingdom as committed to Peter concerned the church, then why would the Lord commit the revelations concerning the church to Paul? The evident truth is that Peter's ministry primarily concerned Israel. It had meaning for the Gentiles only in the sense that the Gentiles are to be blessed through Israel during the Kingdom age.

The mission that the Lord committed to Peter is revealed in the second chapter of Acts, where the great apostle preached his first message to Israel. Of this message, Dr. Arno C. Gaebelien said in his book *The Acts of the Apostles*:

> "...*Here we must not forget that Peter's preaching on the day of Pentecost had to do with the kingdom....Another offer of the kingdom was made to the nation....In this national testimony the word 'repent' stands in the foreground, and their baptism in the name of Him whom they had crucified was a witness that they owned Him now, and believed on Him....The Gospel, in all its blessed fullness as revealed to the great apostle to the Gentiles, Paul, which he called 'my gospel' and as preached by him, makes 'faith'--'believe' as prominent as Peter's preaching 'repent.'*"

There are many scriptures which illustrate the sharp division between the gospel preached by Peter and the leaders of the church at Jerusalem, and the gospel preached by the ministry of Paul. When Paul was preaching the gospel which the Lord had given him for the Gentiles, certain men from the Jerusalem church came down to Antioch and told the new converts, the babes in Christ, that contrary to what Paul had told them, they were not saved by faith alone. They had to be circumcised. For the sake of not having the new Christians confused and frustrated--and his work destroyed--Paul went up to have an understanding with Peter and the elders of the Jerusalem church. He took Barnabas, whom the leaders at the Jerusalem church knew, for reference purposes. Had he not been accompanied by Barnabas, he doubtless would not have been received.

Of this journey Paul later wrote, *"Then fourteen years after I went up again to Jerusalem with Barnabas, and took*

*Titus with me also. And I went up by revelation, and commu-
nicated unto them that gospel which I preach among the
Gentiles, but privately to them which were of reputation, lest by
any means I should run, or had run, in vain"* (Gal. 2:1-2).

It is evident from this scripture that the church at
Jerusalem had no idea what Paul was preaching to the
Gentiles until he went up and explained it to them. Paul
did not go up to Jerusalem to get Peter's approval of his
doctrine. Paul's commission did not come from Peter,
nor was he ordained to the ministry by the Jerusalem
church. He was commissioned directly by the Lord
Jesus Christ, whom he met on the road to Damascus.
Christ told Paul what He wanted him to preach to the
Gentiles. Paul declares this in Galatians 1:11-17: *"But I
certify you, brethren, that the gospel which was preached of me
is not after man. For I neither received it of man, neither was
I taught it, but by the revelation of Jesus Christ. For ye have
heard of my conversation in time past in the Jews' religion, how
that beyond measure I persecuted the church of God, and wasted
it....But when it pleased God, who separated me from my
mother's womb, and called me by his grace, To reveal his Son
in me, that I might preach him among the heathen; immediately
I conferred not with flesh and blood: Neither went I up to
Jerusalem to them which were apostles before me; but I went into
Arabia, and returned again unto Damascus."*

The fact that the gospel of grace and the revelation
of the mystery of the church were initially committed to
Paul is brought out by the apostle to the Gentiles in
Ephesians 3:1-3: *"For this cause I Paul, the prisoner of Jesus
Christ for you Gentiles, If ye have heard of the dispensation of
the grace of God which is given me to you-ward: How that by
revelation he made known unto me the mystery; (as I wrote afore
in few words...)."*

Now some contend that we stop too soon in quoting this scripture concerning the unique revelation and

commission of the gospel of grace to Paul. They say we should go on and quote verses five and six where Paul says, *"Which in other ages was not made known unto the sons of men, as it is now revealed unto his holy apostles and prophets by the Spirit; That the Gentiles should be fellowheirs, and of the same body, and partakers of his promise in Christ by the gospel."*

We should take careful note that here Paul is not saying that this revelation also came to the apostles of the church at Jerusalem before it was given to him, or even at the same time. He is simply recounting what happened when he went up to the church at Jerusalem by revelation and committed to them, or revealed to them, that gospel which Christ had commissioned him to preach among the Gentiles. The Holy Spirit reconciled the ministry of Paul with the ministry of Peter so that this strife might be eliminated and the gospel of grace go to the Gentiles unhindered.

Some might ask: What about the conversion of the household of Cornelius when Peter preached to them the gospel? Was not this the gospel of grace which Peter preached to them? If you will read in Acts 10:42, Peter still preached Christ as the judge or ruler of the living dead. While this is certainly true, Peter was still preaching Christ from a Kingdom age covenant position. The message that Peter preached to this Gentile family is the message that Israel will preach to the nations during the Millennium.

As far as the gospel of grace is concerned, the first time the church at Jerusalem, including Peter, heard it was when Paul went up by revelation and privately revealed it to them.

Chapter Two

God Is a Dispensationalist

Recently, while attending a large church in Oklahoma City, the pastor remarked, "I do not attempt to teach the Bible dispensationally; in fact, I am afraid of dispensationalists." This opinion seems to be that of the vast majority of the clergy today. Yet, failure to interpret the Bible dispensationally opens the doctrinal door to multitudes of false cults and apostasies. For example, it is claimed that over half the Jehovah's Witness movement are former Southern Baptists. The latest in the parade of anti-dispensationalists are the Reconstructionists and Kingdom Now dreamers. These "pied pipers" are leading millions down a one-way, dead-end road of religious futility.

According to *Webster's New World Dictionary*, the primary meanings of "dispense" are:

1. to give or deal out; distribute;
2. to prepare and give out; and
3. to administer.

Thus, a dispensationalist is one who gives, metes out, disseminates, or administers. A dispensation is the time period or era in which such an administration or dissemination is occurring.

The Roman Catholic Church has traditionally interpreted a dispensation to mean the special granting of a privilege for someone to do something that they should not be doing in the first place. The selling of dispensations as per the pope's permission was one thing that incited Martin Luther to rebel against papal authority. However, since we do not agree with the Vatican's use of dispensations, we will move on to the correct biblical teaching.

God's Dispensational Purpose

We read first in Ephesians 1:3-12, *"Blessed be the God and the Father of our Lord Jesus Christ, who hath blessed us with all spiritual blessings in heavenly places in Christ: According as he hath chosen us in him before the foundation of the world, that we should be holy and without blame before him in love: Having predestinated us unto the adoption of children by Jesus Christ to himself, according to the good pleasure of his will, To the praise of the glory of his grace, wherein he hath made us accepted in the beloved. In whom we have redemption through his blood, the forgiveness of sins, according to the riches of his grace; Wherein he hath abounded toward us in all wisdom and prudence; Having made known unto us the mystery of his will, according to his good pleasure which he hath purposed in himself; That in the dispensation of the fulness of times he might gather together in one all things in Christ, both which are in heaven, and which are on earth: even in him: In whom also we have obtained an inheritance, being predestinated according to the purpose of him who worketh all things after the counsel of his own will: That we should be to the praise of his glory, who first trusted in Christ."*

Paul, God's called and appointed apostle to the Gentiles, affirmed that the Creator has a plan and a purpose in His administration over everything in Heaven and on earth. As far as man is concerned, God has purposed to move mankind from point A (Adam and

Eve in the Garden of Eden) to point B (a redeemed body, or congregation, in the New Heaven and the New Earth). Along the road of time from point A to point B, God administers His will and purpose in dispensational periods. The point of the completion of God's purpose with mankind will occur during the dispensation of the fullness of time when everything and everyone will be placed under the dominion of the Lord Jesus Christ. Now it is important to note that Paul stresses in verse four that this plan and purpose was initiated, carried out, and will be consummated in love. God is love; there are at least five hundred scriptures in the Bible which declare God's love for mankind. God's love is manifested in sending His only begotten Son to die for our sins so that in the fullness of time we might become partakers of His glory in eternity.

God is a dispensationalist. He dispenses His mercy, love, and grace in order to fulfill His will. But He also dispenses justice and judgment upon those who knowingly and consciously reject His universal Lordship and way of salvation.

Dispensation of Moral Choice (Innocence)

The dispensational course of biblical history begins with Genesis 1:27-28: *"So God created man in his own image, in the image of God created he him; male and female created he them. And God blessed them, and God said unto them, Be fruitful, and multiply, and replenish the earth, and subdue it: and have dominion over the fish of the sea, and over the fowl of the air, and over every living thing that moveth upon the earth."*

According to Scripture, dispensational truth encompasses the love of God. Just as a woman is glorified by the love of a man, or a man is glorified by the love of a woman, God is glorified in the love of His created, or His children. In Luke 3:38, we read that Adam was created as the son of God by direct creation. The test of love toward the Creator is by keeping His commandments or laws. The base of all dispensational truth is found in the words of Jesus in John 14:15: *"If ye love me, keep my commandments."*

The commandment given to Adam in the first dispensation was quite simple: *"And the Lord God commanded the man, saying, Of every tree of the garden thou mayest freely eat: But of the tree of the knowledge of good and evil, thou shalt not eat of it: for in the day that thou eatest thereof thou shalt surely die"* (Gen. 2:16-17).

Man was created by God and given the right of choice, and in Genesis 3:1-5 we find that Satan entered the scene to tempt man to make the wrong choice. The decision is recorded in Genesis 3:6: *"And when the woman saw that the tree was good for food, and that it was pleasant to the eyes, and a tree to be desired to make one wise, she took of the fruit thereof, and did eat, and gave also unto her husband with her; and he did eat."*

The biblical definition of sin is the transgression of God's law or commandment. Adam knowingly and willingly made a decision not to obey God. It was not that Adam didn't know God. We read in Genesis 3:8 that God would commune and walk with Adam every day. So by one man, Adam, sin entered the world and the sentence of death for disobedience passed upon all mankind from that day to this (1 Cor. 15:22).

One of the most common questions asked by atheists or unbelievers is: Why would an all-knowing God create a being capable of disobedience, who causes all the murder, war, and suffering in the world today? In considering this question, let us suppose that a young man seeks a wife who will love him and be a faithful companion to him for the rest of his life. Of course, he could build a robot, buy a wife (should he live in a nation where this is still legal), or even go out and buy one of those huge plastic dolls. But of what credit, honor, or glory would that be to him? A man or woman desires a helpmate to be a husband or wife because of who they are. We want someone to love us and choose us out of free moral choice. God desires men and women to love Him, be faithful to Him, obey Him, and worship Him because of who He is--their Creator and God. There would be no honor or glory to God to create a being without a choice.

Most theologians and ministers who interpret the Scriptures dispensationally call the first segment of time in God's dealing with men the dispensation of innocence. This is correct in that man was innocent before he sinned. But I think of it as the "dispensation of choice," or "free moral agency." Adam and Eve were given a choice and they made the wrong choice. The penalty for this wrong decision was severe--physical death, cast out of the Garden of Eden, forbidden to eat of the Tree of Life, suffering in child-bearing, earning a livelihood by toil and sweat.

On the dispensational road to fullness of times, God never backtracks on His ultimate will and purpose. We read in Romans 11:29, "For the gifts and calling of God are without repentance."

Dispensation of Conscience

After man made the wrong choice, God added a conscience to help man make the right choice. But God did not take away the freedom of choice. Today each of us is faced with a choice every hour of the day: what time we get up; what food we eat; which clothes we wear;

whether to smoke or not smoke; whether to take drugs or not take drugs; whether to be law-abiding citizens or lawbreakers; whether to be a faithful husband/wife or unfaithful; whether to accept Jesus Christ as Savior or refuse to accept Him. *"For God so loved the world, that he gave his only begotten Son, that whosoever believeth in him should not perish, but have everlasting life" (John 3:16).*

Isn't it wonderful that God created us as free moral agents so that we can make our own decisions; and when a man, woman, or child makes the decision to believe in Jesus Christ, then God is glorified.

Webster's New World Dictionary gives the following definition for "conscience":

> *"Moral sense; a knowledge or sense of right and wrong (good and evil), with a compulsion to do right; moral judgment that opposes the violation of a previously recognized ethical principle and that leads to feelings of guilt if one violates such a principle."*

After Adam and Eve made their decision to disobey God and eat of the Tree of Knowledge of Good and Evil, God gave them a conscience to help make the choice to do good instead of evil. It was a conscience that made Adam and Eve feel guilty because they were naked. They sewed leaves together for a covering to hide their shame. God made them a more substantial covering with animal skins.

There was no covering for sin in the leaves, as we read in Isaiah 64:6: *"But we are all as an unclean thing, and all our righteousnesses are as filthy rags; and we all do fade as a leaf; and our iniquities, like the wind, have taken us away."* The animals killed to provide a covering for sin as dictated by conscience looked forward in type to the ultimate covering for sin, the sacrifice of God's Lamb, the Lord Jesus Christ. *"For if the blood of bulls and of goats, and the ashes of an heifer sprinkling the unclean, sanctifieth to the purifying of the flesh: How much more shall the blood of Christ, who through the eternal Spirit offered himself without spot to God, purge your conscience from dead works to serve the living God"* (Heb. 9:13-14).

Next we consider Adam's first two sons, Cain and Abel. Both had a decision to make as to their justification before God. With a clean conscience Abel made his peace with God in the offering of a lamb. Cain offered to God the fruit of his own labor; but his conscience was not purged of guilt, so he rose up and murdered his brother. Therefore, in the second test of conscience, it was only fifty percent effective. Conscience was not an absolute safeguard; it did not take away the absolute freewill choice. Conscience would convict a man of sin, but it did not necessarily follow that man would always listen to his conscience.

During the second dispensation, God let every man decide for himself what was right in his own eyes, according to conscience. There evidently was no penalty, even for murder, and in due course, conscience develops an immunity. The more frequently a sin is committed, the less guilt the sinner feels. Consequently, we read of the Antediluvian civilization: "And God saw that the wickedness of man was great in the earth, and that every imagination of the thoughts of his heart was only evil continually" (Gen. 6:5). God brought a flood upon the earth that killed a civilization that probably numbered in the billions with only eight souls, Noah and his household, living to repopulate the earth.

But God did not eliminate conscience. We read in Romans 2:14-15 that the Gentiles who were never given the law have no excuse for not keeping the moral intents of the law because God has given them a conscience which warns them when they fail to keep the law. Even as Christians, in scripture after scripture in the epistles, we are admonished to diligently give heed to our conscience in keeping our faith and testimony pure.

Dispensation of Human Government

To choice was added conscience, and again man failed miserably; so to conscience and choice God added human government. The ordinance for human government is found in Genesis 9:5-6: *"And surely your blood of your lives will I require; at the hand of every beast will I require it, and at the hand of man; at the hand of every man's brother will I require the life of man. Whoso sheddeth man's blood, by man shall his blood be shed: for in the image of God made he man."*

Before the flood every man did what was right in his own eyes without fear of retribution. Crime and ungodliness filled the world. There was utter disorder, chaos, and confusion. Therefore, so that His plan and purpose for mankind could go forward once more, God instituted human government. The Divinely-ordained structure for government was that the human race be divided into seventy nations from the three sons of Noah. The rockbed of human government was instituted authority to punish those who would assault, rob, plunder, or rape. The most severe penalty was to be for murder--killing another without reason except for protection of self or property. For this crime the death penalty was demanded.

The reason for God including human government within His plan and purpose is explained in 1 Timothy 2:1-4: *"I exhort therefore, that, first of all, supplications, prayers, intercessions, and giving of thanks, be made for all men: For kings, and for all that are in authority; that we may lead a quiet and peaceable life in all godliness and honesty. For this is good and acceptable in the sight of God our Saviour; Who will have all men to be saved, and to come unto the knowledge of the truth."*

Government was to prevent the universal breakdown of the moral structure of the human race, and to give men at least an opportunity to come to the knowledge of God's will for them to be saved. But from the biblical account in the tenth chapter of Genesis, as well as traditional historical accounts, it would appear that a strong man by the name of Nimrod sought to circumvent God's plan for nations. Nimrod sought to keep all the descendants of Noah under his control, and we read of God's intervention in that situation in Genesis 11:6-8, *"And the Lord said, Behold, the people is one, and they have all one language; and this they begin to do: and now nothing will be restrained from them, which they have imagined to do. Go to, let us go down, and there confound their language, that they may not understand one another's speech. So the Lord scattered them abroad from thence upon the face of all the earth: and they left off to build the city."*

So to free moral agency, or choice, God added conscience, and to conscience He added human government.

Dispensation of Promise

We read in Genesis 10:25 that in the days of Peleg, a great grandson of Shem, the earth was divided. The land mass was all on one continent, and it was broken up, probably due to the breaking up of the foundations of the deep at the flood. This would have been in the years preceding the attempt to build the Tower of

Babel. The Tower of Babel was evidently built to keep the population of the world together instead of having it scattered abroad on continents and islands. But with the confounding of man's speech into many languages, men could not communicate on the project and it was terminated. The races were then divided and scattered around the globe. Geology confirms that the continents and islands can be fitted together again like a jigsaw puzzle.

Paul declared in Acts 17:26-27 that God divided the nations and determined the borders of each nation for the purpose that men might seek knowledge of God and His will. But how and where could they come to know the Lord?

This brings us to another step in the dissemination, or dispensing, of God's will and purpose for mankind, the dispensation of promise. In Genesis 12:1-3, God spoke to a descendant of Shem through Peleg, a man by the name of Abram, or Abraham, living in Ur: *"Now the Lord had said unto Abram, Get thee out of thy country, and from thy kindred, and from thy father's house, unto a land that I will shew thee: And I will make of thee a great nation, and I will bless thee, and make thy name great; and thou shalt be a blessing: And I will bless them that bless thee, and curse him that curseth thee: and in thee shall all families of the earth be blessed."*

The reason we call this ear in God's dispensation "promise" is explained in Hebrews 11:8-9: *"By faith Abraham, when he was called to go out into a place which he should after receive for an inheritance, obeyed; and he went out, not knowing whither he went. By faith he sojourned in the land of promise, as in a strange country, dwelling in tabernacles with Isaac and Jacob, the heirs with him of the same promise."*

Abraham had many descendants, but God's promise of a great nation in which all nations would be blessed was passed to his son Isaac by his legal wife, Sarah, and then on to Isaac's son, Jacob. Jacob was the father of twelve sons from whom came the twelve tribes of Israel. Now, why would Israel, God's nation of promise, become a nation that blesses all others? Because we read in Exodus 19:6; 30:19-21; Numbers 8:5-7,21, and many other scriptures, that Israel was to become a holy nation of priests to the entire world, and lead all nations into the worship of the one true God.

All Abraham had to do to possess the land of promise, the land of Canaan, was to dwell on it. But as great a man of faith as he was, when his faith was tested he went down to Egypt and almost lost his wife, Sarah, who was to bring forth the heir of promise. Still later, when the nation of Israel consisted of only the children and grandchildren of Jacob, during a severe famine the entire family moved to Egypt to obtain food. Here they stayed for four hundred years as prophesied in Genesis 15:13-14: *"And he said unto Abram, Know of a surety that thy seed shall be a stranger in a land that is not their's, and shall serve them; and they shall afflict them four hundred years; And also that nation, whom they shall serve, will I judge: and afterward shall they come out with great substance."*

After four hundred years in bondage, God brought ten plagues upon Egypt and Moses led the Jews out to claim the promised land. How could this undisciplined race of Hebrews who had become idol worshippers, blasphemers, and licentious sinners become a holy nation and fulfill God's will? They had no understanding of the promise made to Abraham, so it was time for God to bring about another dispensational change.

Dispensation of the Law

The fifth dispensation began with Moses descending Mount Sinai with two slabs of stone on which were engraved ten commandments for the Hebrew refugees from Egypt, who were as yet not even a nation. We read in John 1:17, *"For the law was given by Moses, but grace and truth came by Jesus Christ."*

The reason for the law in God's plan and purpose was to bring Israel to a spiritual position whereby the nation would fulfill its mission of becoming priests to the whole world and a blessing to all people. The law encompassed the coming of a Messiah from the lineage of King David to take away sin and assume the responsibility of government upon Himself. The coming of God's Savior, or Messiah, was prophesied in Genesis 3:15, Numbers 24, 2 Samuel 27, many of the Psalms, Isaiah 53, Daniel 9:26, Zechariah 6:12, and other scriptures far too numerous to mention. We read in Galatians 3:24, *"Wherefore the law was our schoolmaster to bring us unto Christ, that we might be justified by faith."*

While the Gentiles may have observed the moral precepts of the law according to conscience, we read in Exodus 20:22 and Romans 9:4 that the letter of the law was given to Israel. Even the keeping of Saturday as the Sabbath was commanded only to Israel.

Besides keeping the commandments and ordinances of the law, the law also entailed a specific order of worship and sacrifice, first in the Tabernacle and later in the Temple. It also encompassed certain food restrictions, dietary rules, and the observance of holy days and feast days. The law itself provided no plan of redemption or salvation. *"Now we know that what things soever the law saith, it saith to them who are under the law: that every mouth may be stopped, and all the world may become guilty before God. Therefore by the deeds of the law there shall no flesh be justified in his sight: for by the law is the knowledge of sin"* (Rom. 3:19-20). As declared in the ninth and tenth chapters of Hebrews, everything commanded in the law, sacrifices within the law, religious observances, feast days, and holy days, pointed Israel to the coming of the Lord Jesus Christ.

When John the Baptist, a type of Elijah and the heralder of the Messiah, appeared on the scene as prophesied by Malachi, he came with a baptism unto repentance. His message was only to Israel: repent, clean up your act, get ready for the Messiah, because the Kingdom of Heaven is at hand. The only problem with the Reconstructionists and the Kingdom Now people of today is that they were born two thousand years too late. When Jesus appeared, He gave evidence to Israel that He was the Messiah. This proof included His message, His miracles, His fulfillment of the messianic prophecies, and finally His resurrection. Jesus came initially only to Israel; He told His apostles to go only to Israel. We read in Romans 15:8, *"Now I say that Jesus Christ was a minister of the circumcision for the truth of God, to confirm the promises made unto the fathers."* Jesus came to Israel to fulfill the promise made to Abraham concerning a nation of priests and to David regarding a messianic King. But the forerunner of Jesus Christ was beheaded, and the vast majority of the nation shouted: *"We will not have this man to rule over us. Crucify him and let his blood be upon us and our children."*

The dispensation of the law ended at the cross (Col. 2:14).

Kingdom Offering Extension

Nevertheless, the Kingdom offer was extended to Israel for forty years after the crucifixion of the Messiah. Forty is the number of testing. Peter declared at what occurred on the day of Pentecost: *"But this is that which was spoken of by the prophet Joel"* (Acts 2:16). But Joel did not prophesy about the church age. Joel prophesied about the Day of the Lord, a time of coming judgment, even upon Israel, with the bringing in of the Kingdom to follow. But Joel also prophesied that Israel should repent and turn to the Lord their God, and perhaps He would come back and repent of the judgment that was determined for the nation. And this was the message that was preached by the apostles. They continued to include baptism as evidence of repentance, and we read in Acts 3:19-20, *"Repent ye therefore, and be converted, that your sins may be blotted out, when the times of refreshing shall come from the presence of the Lord; And he shall send Jesus Christ, which before was preached unto you."*

Upon repentance in Israel and a call by the nation to send Jesus Christ, He would have returned at that time. But the Jewish church at Jerusalem continued to worship at the Temple. When Paul returned to Jerusalem in A.D. 58, James met him with the good news that the membership was diligently following the law, and Paul himself was required to go to the Temple and offer a sacrifice for his sin of instructing the Jews among the Gentiles that they did not have to be circumcised. Circumcision was a sign of the promise of a holy nation. James did not want Paul taking away this promise. But the Kingdom offer was removed completely at the destruction of the Temple in A.D. 70 when Israel ceased to be an identifiable nation. But God had already made provisions for His plan and purpose to proceed in spite of the failure of Israel to know the day of the visitation.

Dispensation of Grace

We read in John 1:11-12, *"He came unto his own, and*

his own received him not. But as many as received him, to them gave he power to become the sons of God, even to them that believe on his name."

According to the covenant that God made with Noah, it was time for the enlargement of Japheth when the descendants of Japheth should live in the tents of Shem, but how would the Gentile world be blessed through the promise of Abraham? The answer is provided in Ephesians 3:1-6: *"For this cause I Paul, the prisoner of Jesus Christ for you Gentiles, If ye have heard of the dispensation of the grace of God which is given me to you-ward: How that by revelation he made known unto me the mystery; (as I wrote afore in few words, Whereby, when ye read, ye may understand my knowledge in the mystery of Christ) Which in other ages was not made known unto the sons of men, as it is now revealed unto his holy apostles and prophets by the Spirit; That the Gentiles should be fellowheirs, and of the same body, and partakers of his promise in Christ by the gospel."*

The Gentiles did not have the law, circumcision, a Temple in Jerusalem, or any promise to be partakers with Israel in blessings from God. The only notice to them from God was that they could become Jewish proselytes, a promise to dwell in the tents of Shem, to be blessed by the national priesthood of Israel, and to come to the light of Israel's Messiah in the Kingdom age. So God sent forth Paul with a message of God's sovereign grace, a mystery that was completely hidden and unknown. Anyone, Jew or Gentile, could be saved by faith in Jesus Christ who died for the sins of the world. Race didn't matter; age didn't matter; sex didn't matter; only faith by grace resulting in a new birth by the Holy Spirit into the family of God mattered. *"For by grace are ye saved through faith; and that not of yourselves: it is the gift of God: Not of works, lest any man should boast"* (Eph. 2:8-9).

Of the dispensation of grace, which is the hidden dispensation of mystery, we read in Acts 15:14-16, *"...God at the first did visit the Gentiles, to take out of them a people for his name. And to this agree the words of the prophets; as it is written, After this I will return, and will build again the tabernacle of David: which is fallen down; and I will build again the ruins thereof, and I will set it up."* According to this prophecy, the dispensation of grace came with the passing of Israel as a nation and the dispersion of the Jews. It will end with the refounding of Israel as a nation and their regathering (Rom. 11). The fullness, or completion of the Gentile church age occurs at the translation of the church body to Heaven (1 Thess. 4:13-18). This translation is also called the Rapture.

In a sense, the sixth dispensation, the dispensation of grace, ends with another failure of man: apostasy within Christendom; population explosion with added billions going to Hell; as in Noah's day, crime and perversion filling the earth; and man himself threatening to destroy the world (1 Tim. 4:1-2; 2 Tim. 3:1-9; 2 Pet. 2-3; Matt. 24:37; Rev. 11:18).

The Kingdom Age (Millennium)

Jesus said of the end of the age, *"For then shall be great tribulation, such as was not since the beginning of the world to this time, no, nor ever shall be"* (Matt. 24:21). All the prophets from Moses to Joel and Zechariah foretold the judgments coming upon the world during this period. According to Daniel and the Apostle John, this time of world tribulation will last for seven years; and as we understand it, it will start immediately after the Rapture of the church. It will be concluded with the visible return of Jesus Christ with the armies of Heaven (Rev. 19; Matt. 24:27). He will rebuild the Temple and establish His administration from Heaven in accordance with the prophecies of Ezekiel and Zechariah.

The ecology of the earth will revert back to the Antediluvian age and men will again live eight or nine hundred years. Jesus Christ Himself will reign on David's throne (Luke 1:32-33). The law will be enforced over all the earth; nations will beat their armaments into agricultural implements; nature will be at peace because sin has been restrained. The twelve apostles will be governors over the twelve tribes of Israel (Matt. 19:28; Rev. 20:4). Israel will become a nation of priests to all the world, and the Gentile nations will bring a tithe of their gross national product to Jerusalem. Satan, who has intervened with mankind to subvert every dispensation, will be bound for a thousand years. Five times we are informed in Revelation 20 that the Kingdom dispensation will continue for one thousand years. During the messianic administration the orders for all former dispensations will be fulfilled: grace will come from the presence of the Lord Jesus Christ; the government will be upon His shoulders; the nations will have their rulers under the benevolent Kingship of Jesus; there will be absolute law and justice; Israel will fulfill God's promise. But now comes the choice. What will the nations do when Satan is loosed for a little season? Once again man makes the wrong choice. The nations rise up once more to destroy the Lord Jesus Christ and His saints (Rev. 20:7-9).

New Heaven and New Earth

The eighth dispensation is the New Heaven and the New Earth. Eight is the number of new beginnings. After God rested on the seventh day, the eighth day signified the operation of all creation.

The resurrection of all the saved is completed with the first resurrection at the beginning of the Kingdom age; the resurrection of the lost and their eternal judgment takes place at the end of the Kingdom age. Then we read that God will create a New Heaven and a New Earth.

Within the New Heaven and the New Earth there will be only those who have made the right choice--to believe God and accept His only way of salvation, His only begotten Son, the Lord Jesus Christ. A man's conscience will never bother him again because there will be no sin committed (Rev. 21:8). Israel will be the center of the nations and the twelve gates of the New Jerusalem will be named for the twelve tribes. The saved of the Kingdom age will comprise the nations of the New Earth. As Jesus told His disciples, love will be the fulfillment of the law and God will love the inhabitants of the New Earth and New Jerusalem forever because they have chosen Him and they will forever keep His eternal commandments. This will be the dispensation of the fullness of time when all things, both in Heaven and in earth, will be placed under the authority of the Lord Jesus Christ. The will and purpose of God within the dispensation of time will be completed.

We read in Revelation 22:17, *"And the Spirit and the bride say, Come. And let him that heareth say, Come. And let him that is athirst come. And whosoever will, let him take the water of life freely."*

God has a plan and a purpose for you, but you have to make the decision. The choice is yours.

Chapter Three

Rightly Dividing the Word

In this study it is of supreme importance to recognize and acknowledge the Lord Jesus Christ as the central theme of the Bible. The Apostle John gave as the reason for the writing of his book, *"But these are written, that ye might believe that Jesus is the Christ, the Son of God; and that believing ye might have life through his name"* (John 20:31). This is not only the reason for the Gospel of John, it is the bedrock foundation of each and every one of the sixty-six books of the Bible.

Had Adam not fallen into sin and brought condemnation upon the whole human race, there would have been no need for the Bible. God would have continued to come down from Heaven as He did with Adam. He would have talked with men personally, and revealed all things to them. But the Scriptures inform us that God cannot look upon sin; therefore, God had to reach man through other avenues of communication. The Bible tells us that He spoke to man through signs, visions, dreams, types, symbols, the law, the prophets, the written Word, and of course, in these last days He has spoken to us directly through Christ Jesus. But in all these myriads of communications, God spoke only of the redemption of man from a lost condition and of the saving of the world from the power of Satan. Paul tells us in Galatians 3:24 that the *"...law was our schoolmaster to bring us unto Christ, that we might be justified by faith."*

God spoke to Adam and Eve of the coming Redeemer in the coats of animal skins that He provided for them. The Holy Spirit convicted Cain that he was a sinner, and he offered an atonement for his sins in the firstlings of his flock. The offering of Abel looked forward in type to the Lamb of God, the Lord Jesus Christ, who was to make an offering for sins, once for all. The ark that carried Noah and his household over the judgment of the flood spoke of the great salvation that God has provided in His Son. Every item in the tabernacle in some way spoke to Israel of the coming Messiah. Even the brazen serpent that Moses lifted up in the wilderness spoke of the Lord Jesus Christ, who would be lifted up on the cross for the sins of the world, as we read in John 3:14. The experience of Jonah in the belly of the whale represented the conquest of Christ over the grave, as we read in Matthew 12:40.

Paul likens the two-fold project of God in the redemption of man and the salvation of the world to the building of a house in Ephesians 2:19-22, built on Jesus, the chief cornerstone, around which all the different components of the building fit neatly together, the foundation being the apostles and prophets. If you were building a house, you would not get a company that specializes in concrete foundation work to do the interior decorating. You would not get a man who specializes in cabinet making to put on the roof, nor would you hire a bricklayer to do the electrical wiring. You would hire the right man for the right job. God is no different in the building of His house. What if Noah, when God told him to build an ark, had taken his family up on Mount Sinai? The flood would have risen even over the top of that mountain and Noah and his household would have drowned. What if Abraham had lacked the faith to leave his country and sojourn in a strange land? What if Lot had not been called out of Sodom? What if Moses, instead of going up on Mount Sinai to receive the law as God commanded, had gone down into the valley and built an ark?

The important thing for us to recognize is that while all things pertaining to the redemption of man and the saving of the world, as given in the Bible, either point to or are built around Christ, God has given each generation, and to specific leaders, different jobs or missions. While some men like Jonah lacked faith to accomplish that which God had told them to do, in the end, the task was accomplished in spite of their weakness. God often uses the weakness in men to show forth His glory. Although Israel failed miserably in the mission that God gave them, namely to become the nucleus for a kingdom of nations upon earth, this plan and purpose of God will yet be accomplished during the Kingdom age. The fact that Israel today has been refounded as a nation is evidence that God intends to fulfill His covenants with Abraham, Isaac, and Jacob. But we must understand that the mission which God has entrusted to us during the dispensation of grace is different from that of Abel; it is different from that of Noah, Abraham, Moses, Isaiah, Daniel, or even the twelve apostles. Jesus said in Matthew 15:24, "...*I am not sent but unto the lost sheep of the house of Israel.*" Although the things which Jesus said and did are important to the Gentile church and are for our edification, instruction, and enlightenment, the ministry of Christ in the flesh was directed toward Israel in the fulfillment of the covenants and the bringing in of the Kingdom. He chose twelve men to help Him in this mission and He called them His apostles. He promised them that in the Kingdom they would sit upon twelve thrones, ruling over the twelve tribes of Israel. Certainly the twelve apostles did not receive this reward during the ministry of our Lord at His first appearing, neither did they receive it during the Pentecostal church age, but to say that they will not receive it is to make Christ a liar. The twelve apostles will receive this duly promised authority during the institution of Christ's authority over the nations at His second appearing, as we read in Revelation 20:4: *"And I saw thrones, and they sat upon them, and judgment was given unto them...."*

This simple truth is to remind you just why we wrote this book. The reason we have so many diverse Christian doctrines, churches, and denominations is that so-called spokesmen of God down through the centuries of the church age have continually tried to give the right people the wrong job. The trouble so many pastors, ministers, evangelists, and theologians have in reconciling the ministry of Paul with the ministry of Peter is in not recognizing the simple truth that Jesus Christ gave them different jobs. The acceptance of this simple fact is the beginning of New Testament understanding.

It would be well for us to prayerfully consider these instructions on *Rightly Dividing the Word and Dispensational Truths*, written by the late Clarence Larkin:

> *"Writing to Timothy, Paul said: 'Study to shew thyself approved of God, a workman that needeth not to be ashamed, rightly dividing the Word of Truth' (2 Tim. 2:15). The student of the 'Word of God' is here spoken of as a 'workman.' A workman cannot intelligently do his work without a plan. He must have drawings and specifications. God said to Moses as to the Tabernacle, 'See that you make all things according to the Pattern shewed to thee in the mount' (Heb. 8:5). The student of God's Word must under-*

stand God's Plan and Purpose in the Ages, or there will be confusion in his work of interpreting the scriptures.

"While the 'Word of Truth' is written for all classes of people, and for our learning, it is not addressed to all people in general, but part of it is addressed to the Jews, part to the Gentiles, and part to the Church. These three constitute the Three Classes into which humanity is divided (1 Cor. 10:32). It follows therefore, that while the whole Bible was written for the instruction of the Church, it is not all written about the Church. The Church is not mentioned in the Old Testament. It was hid from the Old Testament prophets, and was a 'Mystery' first revealed to Paul, and disclosed by him in Ephesians 3:1-10. The Old Testament is mostly taken up with the history of one nation, that of Israel....When we take the Old Testament promises and apply them to the Church we rob the Jew of that which is exclusively his....In the New Testament, the Epistles of Hebrews and James are Jewish. The Epistle of James is addressed, not to the Church, but to the 'Twelve Tribes scattered abroad.'...In the Epistle to the Hebrews, many Christians stumble at the words 'fall away' (Heb. 6:4-6), and 'if we sin wilfully' (Heb. 10:26). But these words do not apply to Christians. They were spoken to apostate Jewish professors of Christianity who had never been born again, and who, if they did not accept Jesus as their Messiah, practically crucified Him again, and were as bad as their brethren who did crucify Him.

"In 'Rightly Dividing the Word of Truth,' we must also distinguish the work of Christ. We are told in the scriptures that He is a 'Prophet,' 'Priest,' and 'King.' But He does not hold those offices conjointly, but successively. From the Fall in Eden to the Cross, He was a 'Prophet.' He is now a 'High Priest' and when He comes again, He will be a 'King.' From Eden to the Cross there was an 'Altar,' from the Cross to the Crown, there is a 'Table' (the Lord's Table), and from the Crown to Christ's surrender of the Kingdom, there is a 'Throne.'

"In Hebrews 1:1, we read God hath spoken at 'Sundry Times,' as well as in 'Divers Manners,' and if we are to understand what He has spoken, we must not only distinguish between the classes of people He has spoken to, as the Jews, Gentiles, or the Church, but we must also note the 'Sundry Times' at which He spoke, and the 'Divers Manners.' We must also distinguish between the 'Times Past' when He spoke by the Prophets, and these 'Last Days' in which He has spoken to us by His Son....We must also distinguish between the 'Times' and 'Seasons' of the scriptures. Daniel said of God: 'He changeth the Times and the Seasons' (Dan. 2:21), and Jesus said to His disciples: 'It is not for you to know the Times or the Seasons' (Acts 1:7). Job testified that 'Times are not hidden from the Almighty' (Job 24:1)....By the 'Seasons' we are to understand the climatic changes of the earth due to the movements and changing characteristics of the Sun, Moon, and Stars, which God ordained to regulate the 'Seasons' (Gen. 1:14). As to the 'Times' we have them designated as the 'Times of Ignorance' (Acts 17:30); the 'Times of the Gentiles' (Luke 21:24); the 'Times of Refreshing' (Acts 3:19); the 'Times of Restitution' (Eph. 1:10). From the statement, 'the Times of the Gentiles,' we see that when the 'Gentiles' are in power the 'Jews' are not. And as the 'Times of the Gentiles' is still running, the Church cannot be a governing or Kingdom power."

Not long ago, I was having a discussion with a dear Christian lady concerning the importance of our knowing exactly what God has said to us, and she replied: "I just read the words of Jesus and try to live by them." Of course, she meant the words of Jesus as recorded in the four gospels--Matthew, Mark, Luke, and John. What this dear, sweet soul did not understand was that she could not possibly live by all the words that Jesus spoke. The vast majority of the words that Jesus spoke were meant for Israel, not for you, me, nor any other Gentile. I will certainly admit that John appropriated the ministry of Jesus Christ in its worldwide application, but John did not write his gospel until A.D. 90, after the Temple had been destroyed and the covenants with Israel set aside. But especially in Matthew, Mark, and Luke, we must always first look for a primary application to the teachings of Jesus to Israel, for He openly declared that He had come unto none save Israel. This truth is brought out most plainly in Romans 15:8: :8: *"Now I say that Jesus Christ was a minister of the circumcision for the truth of God, to confirm the promises made unto the fathers."*

We must accept this scripture as truth or deny the Bible as the inspired Word of God. The truth expounded here, and also by our Lord in the gospels, is that during the days of His first appearing on earth, He ministered to Israel. He did not minister to the Gentiles. Upon His rejection by Israel as the Messiah, in subsequent crucifixion He took the sins of the whole world upon Himself and was judged before God for all men. But Christ had already given the keys to the Kingdom to Peter. He told Peter and the twelve apostles, whom He called also to be ministers of the Circumcision, to go to Israel and relate to the Jews what this event meant to them according to the covenants. Had Israel received this gospel and believed, then it would have gone out from Jerusalem into all the world. But because Israel again hardened their hearts, the gospel that Peter preached began to decline. After the fifteenth chapter of Acts, Peter is hardly mentioned. Why? Because Jesus Christ called Paul to begin a new ministry, a distinct ministry to the Gentiles. Peter was a minister to the Circumcision, but Paul was a minister to the Gentiles. Paul said that Christ had revealed to him what was to be preached to the Gentiles. We should be particularly interested in the Pauline epistles, for in them we find what God has said to us; what plan and purpose He has for our lives; the future He has planned for us in Heaven; and what He wants us to do while here on earth.

Chapter Four

The Ministry of Peter

Jesus Christ, at His first appearing in the flesh, came to none save the House of Israel. During the three and a half years of His earthly ministry, He ministered or preached to the Jews. He came to preach to Israel and to reveal Himself to the House of David as the promised Messiah who would fulfill the covenants that God made to the fathers of Israel.

Paul declared that Jesus was a minister to the Circumcision, or Israel. God has made certain promises to Israel in the covenants with Abraham, Isaac, Jacob, and David. I will not outline these covenants, for they should be common knowledge to any Christian with a minimal knowledge of the Scriptures. Briefly, they encompassed Israel as the chosen people of God, a holy nation on earth, to become God's witness in the world to all nations. All covenants pointed toward an era of peace, plenty, and righteousness on earth through a kingdom of nations in which Israel would be the head. This Kingdom from Heaven, referred to as the "Times of Refreshing," would be brought in by the Messiah, a son of David, who would reign and rule over Israel in Jerusalem.

John the Baptist, in the spirit of Elijah, went before Jesus to announce to Israel that the Messiah was coming and this Kingdom by which He would bring Heaven to earth was near. *"In those days came John the Baptist, preaching in the wilderness of Judea, and saying, Repent ye: for the kingdom of heaven is at hand"* (Matt. 3:1-2).

The beginning of Jesus' ministry to Israel is located in Matthew 4:17: *"From that time Jesus began to preach, and to say, Repent: for the kingdom of heaven is at hand."* From that time forward to the cross, Jesus Christ never deviated from this ministry which the Father had committed to Him. He taught His disciples to pray: *"Thy kingdom come; thy will be done in earth, as it is in heaven"* (Matt. 6:10). He multiplied the loaves and the fishes as a sign to Israel of the blessings awaiting them in the Kingdom; He healed the sick as a sign that He was the One who would rise with healing in His wings; He raised the dead to reveal to Israel that He was the resurrection and the life; all these and many other wonderful things He did. But they were given as signs to Israel that He was the Messiah who would bring down the Kingdom from Heaven to earth. In the fifteenth chapter of Matthew, it is recorded that a poor Canaanite mother came to Jesus begging Him to heal her daughter who was possessed with a devil. With tears streaming down her face, she cried, "Lord help me." But we read that Jesus answered her not one word. He ignored her. And when she continued to cry, He turned to her and said, *"I am not sent but unto the house of the lost sheep of Israel....It is not meet to take the children's bread, and to cast it to dogs."* Of course, because of the mother's faith, Jesus did heal her child, but the Lord first had to make it perfectly clear, not only to this Gentile, but also to the Jewish disciples, that He had come to minister to none but Israel.

Even the Olivet Discourse had no application to the church, except that in the refounding of Israel and fulfilling of the many prophecies as they relate to the new nation of Israel, Christians know that the end of the church age is near and our gathering together to meet the Lord in the air is even at the door. It is very important for us to study the Olivet Discourse, just as it is for us to study all of the gospels. But the Olivet Discourse was not directed to Christians. It concerns the destruction of Jerusalem and the Jewish Temple; it concerns the dispersion of the Jews into all nations of the world for many days; it concerns their regathering into the land and the refounding of Israel as a nation; it concerns the time of Jacob's trouble, or Israel's troubles during the Great Tribulation; and it concerns the second appearing of Christ to Israel, not as a lowly minister and prophet, but as the glorified Messiah, the King of kings and Lord of lords.

It is of the greatest importance to our study to note that in spite of the miracles of Jesus, and the many other signs that He gave to Israel during the three and a half years from His baptism to the cross, His ministry to Israel was not completed with the internment of His body in the tomb. Certainly, the evidence that Jesus presented to Israel proved without any doubt that He was the Messiah, but there were other prophecies that the prophets had made allowance for in their writings, and some of these definitely concerned the ministry of Peter. The unfulfilled prophecies concerning the Messiahship of Jesus up to the time He was taken to Calvary were:

1. The sins of the world were to be laid upon Him and He was to be smitten of God for them (Isa. 53:4).
2. He had to be wounded for the transgressions of the world and die a violent death (Isa. 53:5).
3. He was to be laid in a rich man's tomb (Isa. 53:9).
4. The sign of Jonah was to be given to Israel. The

Messiah was to rise from the grave after three days and three nights (Matt. 12:40; Isa. 53:9-10). Josephus recognized that the resurrection of Christ from the grave was doubtless the greatest sign given to Israel that Jesus was the Messiah. Quoting the renowned Jewish historian: *"And when Pilate, at the suggestion of the principal men amongst us, had condemned Him to the cross, those that loved Him at the first did not forsake Him; for He appeared to them alive again the third day; as the divine prophets had foretold these and ten thousand other wonderful things concerning Him."*

5. The Messiah was to be cut off from Israel according to Daniel, and the fact that His first coming would be separated from His second coming by a period of time is listed in innumerable scriptures in Isaiah and other prophetic books.

6. The Holy Spirit poured out upon the sons and daughters of Israel (Joel 2:28; Zech. 12:10).

These final prophetic proofs had to be presented to Israel as a sign that Jesus was in truth the Messiah. Jesus chose the apostle most representative of Israel to present this second offer of the Kingdom to Israel. He presented to Peter the keys to the Kingdom. Peter--faithful at times and backsliding at others, courageous and cowardly, boastful and timid, running hot and cold--was so typical of the national character of Israel. However, when the Holy Spirit fell upon Peter and the rest of the Jewish disciples at Pentecost, all the weaknesses in Peter's nature were overcome by his finer qualities. What happened to Peter at Pentecost is representative of what will happen to all of Israel when Christ returns.

That Christ did give Peter the keys to the Kingdom is indeed fact. That Peter was recognized as the primal head of the Pentecostal church is without question. His position in this early assembly of disciples is clearly set forth in the first few chapters of Acts. That Peter was the head of the Jerusalem church is also beyond doubt, for he is so declared by Paul in Acts, and in several of his epistles.

We now arrive at a critical point in our study of this subject: What did Peter preach? What specific mission did Christ give to Peter?

We find a clue to what Peter preached and the nature of his mission in Luke 24:47: *"And that repentance and remission of sins should be preached in his name among all nations, beginning at Jerusalem."* It is unthinkable that Peter would have preached anything else. This message which the apostles and disciples were to preach is the same as that gospel which must be published among all nations (Mark 13:10). However, when we speak of gospel, we do not necessarily mean the gospel of grace. The New Testament speaks of two gospels: the gospel of grace and the gospel of the Kingdom. *Gospel* in the original Greek text simply means "glad tidings" or "good news." Peter preached the gospel and Paul preached the gospel, yet this does not necessarily mean that they preached the same message. Peter had glad tidings for Israel and Paul had glad tidings for the Gentiles.

The apostles, under the leadership of Peter were commanded by Jesus to first preach the gospel in Jerusalem and then to all nations. The meaning here is strong and clear. The Gentiles were to be saved through Jewish apostles and disciples as Christ would be preached unto them according to the covenants of Israel--the law would go forth from Jerusalem, the Messiah would be a light to the Gentiles, and all nations would look toward Jerusalem for spiritual leadership. This gospel that Peter and the apostles and disciples preached hinged upon the bringing in of the Kingdom, and in turn was contingent upon the acceptance by Israel of Christ as the promised Messiah. To Israel, Peter was acting in Christ's place. Both Christ and Peter are listed in the scriptures as ministers to the Circumcision, or Israel. Both preached the same gospel to Israel. Christ preached: *"Repent, for the kingdom of heaven is at hand."* Peter preached, as recorded in Acts 3:19-20: *"Repent ye therefore, and be converted, that your sins may be blotted out, when the times of refreshing* [the Kingdom of Heaven] *shall come from the presence of the Lord; And he shall send Jesus Christ, which before was preached unto you."* Peter preached that if Israel would repent and receive Christ as Lord, God would send Him back to bring in the Kingdom. Peter's message envisioned a return of Christ upon repentance in Israel to personally blot out their sins.

Chapter Five

Pentecostal Power

Peter was honored above the other eleven apostles in that Christ chose him to receive the keys of the Kingdom. Peter is recognized as the spokesman for the twelve, and later as the chief pillar of the Jerusalem church. After Pentecost, Peter naturally began to fulfill the mission which God had given him. Peter began to preach to Israel.

Inasmuch as the ministries of Peter and Paul were separate, the Gentile church bodies must either claim all of what Peter preached, or all of what Paul preached. They should not claim both. Yet all major denominations want to claim part of what Peter preached, but none dare claim all of his gospel. Churches will mix part of what Peter preached with part of what Paul preached, claiming only those doctrinal points which fit their theology. This is why we have had so many doctrines, sects, and denominations since the days of Paul. If all had strictly followed Peter, there would have been no division. If all had espoused the gospel of Paul, the same would have been true.

Now, let us analyze this "gospel of the Circumcision" which Peter preached. We find Peter's first sermon recorded in the second chapter of Acts, beginning with verse fourteen: *"But Peter, standing up with the eleven, lifted up his voice, and said unto them, Ye men of Judaea, and all ye that dwell at Jerusalem, be this known unto you and hearken to my words: For these are not drunken, as ye suppose, seeing it is but the third hour of the day. But this is that which was spoken by the prophet Joel; And it shall come to pass in the last days, saith God, I will pour out of my Spirit upon all flesh; and your sons and your daughters shall prophesy, and your young men shall see visions, and your old men shall dream dreams; And on my servants and on my handmaidens I will pour out in those days of my Spirit; and they shall prophesy; and I will shew wonders in heaven above, and signs in the earth beneath; blood, and fire, and vapour of smoke: The sun shall be turned into darkness, and the moon into blood, before that great and notable day of the Lord come. And it shall come to pass, that whosoever shall call on the name of the Lord shall be saved."*

To whom did Peter preach? He preached to the Circumcision, Israel. Did he preach to any Gentiles? No, only to the men of Judea and those who dwelled at Jerusalem. What did he preach first? At the beginning, he preached the message of Joel concerning the pouring out of the Spirit upon Israel at the coming of the Messiah in the notable day of the Lord when all Gentile power and authority would be put down and the Kingdom from Heaven would be brought in. All the prophecies concerning the Messiah had to be fulfilled before Israel's eyes. The pouring out of the Spirit at Pentecost was one that had not been fulfilled as yet.

Did this concern the Gentile church? No, it did not. How can I be so positive? Because Paul said in Ephesians 3:1-6 that the revelation concerning the church was not made known unto the sons of men of any former age. The Old Testament prophets of Israel knew nothing about the church. Joel knew nothing about the church or the gospel of grace, yet Peter said what happened at Pentecost was that which had been prophesied by Joel. The question we must pose is why Gentile Christians try to claim what happened at Pentecost to the disciples as a distinct gift from God to them, when this event was clearly a fulfillment of a sign to Israel that the Day of the Lord was at hand.

As to the significance of the gospel of the Kingdom, as preached by Peter on the day of Pentecost and its relation to the gospel preached by Paul, let us consider the following:

God chose one man, Abraham, to establish a nation that might be His witness in the world and take the Word of God to all men. Abraham originally spoke the Chaldean language, but he developed a new language which would serve as a base whereby he could communicate God's will and Word to other races. This language was the Hebrew language, and it was doubtless given to Abraham by the Holy Spirit, as it is the most heavenly language on earth--beautiful, flowing, and symphonic. Christ prophesied in the Olivet Discourse that the gospel of the Kingdom would be preached to all nations for a witness; and it will, but preached only by Israelites. This mass communicating of God's message to all men will be accomplished by an outpouring of the Spirit, as explained in Joel 2:28 and many other scriptures. God's Word cannot be proclaimed except men be led of the Spirit to understand it.

The commission given to the apostles and the early Jewish church was to go into all the world preaching the gospel of the Kingdom, but their mission was to begin at Jerusalem (they knew nothing of the gospel of grace at that time). Had Israel received and believed the Gospel concerning Jesus Christ according to the covenants, God would have sent Jesus Christ back at that time as Peter promised to Israel in Acts 3:19. Because Israel as a nation still rejected Christ as the Messiah who would bring in the Kingdom of Heaven, the apostles were bound to their first order and they remained ministers to the Circumcision (Israel) all their lives. To contend that the Apostle Paul and the twelve apostles at Jerusalem preached the same gospel is only to display one's misunderstanding of the inspired Word. The church at Jerusalem didn't even know what Paul preached until he went up to Jerusalem as recorded in Acts 15, and explained it to them. Of this conference, Paul said in Galatians 2:2, *"And I went up by revelation [of the Holy Spirit], and communicated unto them that gospel which I preach among the Gentiles...."*

As God prepared the apostles and the early disciples of the Jewish church to go into all the world (from Jerusalem) and preach the Gospel to all nations (of many languages), it is evident they would have to be equipped for their mission. We read in Acts 2:7 that every single disciple gathered together on the day of Pentecost was a *Galilean*. The aristocratic Judeans spoke at least three languages, but the poor and backward Galileans could hardly speak their own--Hebrew. In order to complete their mission to other nations, they would, of necessity, have to speak in other tongues (languages).

*"And when the day of Pentecost was fully come, they were all with one accord in one place. And suddenly there came a sound from heaven as of a rushing mighty wind, and it filled all the house where they were sitting. And there appeared unto them cloven tongues like as of fire, and it sat upon each of them. And they were all filled with the Holy Ghost, and began to speak with other tongues, as the **Spirit gave them utterance**"* (Acts 2:1-4). There is nothing strange or mysterious about this outpouring of the Spirit if we will just let God's Word stand as it is. They simply preached the Word-- the gospel of the Kingdom--to Jews from eighteen foreign nations that had returned to Israel as a sign that

this was that which was prophesied concerning the promise of the Kingdom of God, preparing Israel to go into all the world and preach this Gospel. Endowed with spiritual powers of communication by the Holy Spirit, these ignorant men (according to Judean standards) spoke fluently eighteen different languages. Some were so difficult that even the Romans had not been able to master them. They did not need an interpreter, for this was a true manifestation of the Holy Ghost power that was promised to Israel, as it will later come upon all Israel when Christ returns and is enthroned upon the throne of David.

This Holy Ghost power continued to be extended to Jewish disciples, and even to the Jewish proselyte Cornelius, as a sign that the offer of the Kingdom was still in effect, but God allowed it to go no further, as Israel more and more turned their backs in unbelief, and began to kill and persecute the disciples. It was then that God sent Paul abroad with the gospel of grace, establishing churches in each country, town, and community where each local assembly could be a witness to the saving power of Jesus Christ to their own people. The offer of the Kingdom was gradually set aside along with the ministry of Israel, which was to go into all the world in the power of the Holy Ghost, witnessing to all peoples, nations, and tongues. The authority given by the Holy Ghost, whereby the disciples might speak in other languages was gradually withdrawn as the destruction of Jerusalem and the Temple approached.

There is no evidence in any of the Pauline epistles that any Gentile Christian was ever given this power or authority under the commission of grace. This outpouring of the Spirit unto common universal communication is an entity of the Kingdom of Heaven and is in no way connected with the gospel of grace. Because

Israel rejected this great Kingdom age sign, the Jews themselves would be preached to by people with stammering tongues (Isa. 28:11; 33:19). In comparison to the Hebrew, all Gentile languages are harsh and stammering.

There is no such thing as an unknown tongue given by the power of the Holy Ghost, according to modern interpretation. Of what good would it be in the universal purpose and plan of God? In all references in the fourteenth chapter of 1 Corinthians to the "unknown tongue," the word "unknown" is in italics, indicating that it was not in the original Greek text. The ability to speak in a diversity of tongues is definitely a spiritual gift and of great benefit to Christian missionaries to communicate with the heathen the gospel of grace.

The church at Corinth was the most spiritually confused church mentioned in the New Testament. It misappropriated every basic fundamental of the faith. Paul charged them as being still "babes in Christ." They were "yet carnal" and Paul could preach nothing to their spiritual understanding save "Jesus Christ, and him crucified." One of their great faults was in confusing their ability to speak in other languages with Pentecostal power. Paul exposed their folly as he wrote to them in 1 Corinthians 14:13: *"Wherefore let him that speaketh in an [unknown] tongue pray that he may interpret."* To speak in a foreign language is one thing; to interpret it in another language is quite another. The disciples at Pentecost needed no interpreter and the Holy Spirit never does, for as Paul declares in 1 Timothy 4:1, *"...the spirit speaketh expressly...."* He always has and He always will. Unbelievers at Pentecost had no trouble understanding the disciples, while the unbelievers at Corinth who came to that church thought the members were mad because there was so much confusion in the assembly (1 Cor. 14:19). Paul informed the Corinthians that he spake in tongues more than any of them, and he did. He would preach to the different people that he witnessed to in his missionary journeys. If speaking in tongues, or other languages, is proof of ultimate spirituality and sanctification, why did Paul write that he struggled to keep his body under subjection lest he become a castaway?

Paul explained in 1 Corinthians 14:22 that "...*tongues are for a sign, not to them that believe, but to them that believe not....*" Paul makes it very clear in the twenty-eighth chapter of Acts that it is Israel that believes not, and the Gentiles who would hear and believe. The gift of tongues by Holy Ghost power was another sign to Israel at Pentecost that the Kingdom was being offered by God at that time, and the preaching of the Gospel to Israel in languages other than Hebrew by Gentiles (1 Cor. 14:21) is also a sign to Israel--that the Kingdom has been set aside until the Lord Jesus Christ returns.

Thus we see by properly appropriating the gift of speaking in tongues to Peter's ministry--the gospel of the kingdom--and divorcing it from Paul's ministry--the gospel of grace to the Gentiles--we resolve one of the major doctrinal issues that separates or divides segments of Christendom into various church bodies and denominations.

Chapter Six

Water Baptism--Sink or Swim

It should be self-evident that the Pentecostal churches, the Methodists, the Baptists, the Lutherans, the Presbyterians, and the Episcopalians cannot all interpret, for example, the baptism of the believer differently, and all be right.

I have no illusions that we will to any great degree influence greater understanding and brotherhood among the churches. If Paul could not accomplish Christian unity in his day, our chances today are infinitely less. Paul lamented at the close of his ministry: *"All the churches in Asia have turned against me."* Paul outlined the great frustrator of the gospel of grace that divided Christians, in Galatians 1:7-8: *"...but there be some that trouble you, and would pervert the gospel of Christ. But though we, or an angel from heaven, preach any other gospel unto you [Gentiles] than that which we have preached unto you, let him be accursed."*

This other gospel that was preached to the Galatians, as Paul brings out throughout this epistle, was that which was preached unto them by those who came down from the church at Jerusalem. Peter got into trouble when he went down and tried to instruct the Christians at Antioch. Paul got into trouble when he ignored the warnings of the Spirit and went back up to the Temple at Jerusalem; Christians have been getting into trouble ever since, because they have not rightly divided the Word.

In discussing the second part of Peter's first sermons to Israel it is important to note that the ministry of the early Pentecostal Jerusalem church revolved around the Temple (Acts 2:46). The messianic promise to Israel concerning the opening of the doors of the Kingdom was when the Lord would suddenly come to His Temple. Peter and the disciples had every right to expect the Lord to return to the Temple upon the acceptance of the Gospel which he preached to Israel. This is why the Temple continued to be the center of their activity.

After Peter declared the pouring out of the Spirit, and the disciples talking in other languages, as the sign of the Kingdom prophesied by Joel, he next called the attention of Israel to the sign given by David in chapters one through seventeen of 2 Samuel and chapter one hundred ten of Psalms. This sign, given by the patriarch David, was that God would not let the Holy One of Israel, the Messiah, see corruption, but would be raised from the grave and seated at the right hand of God until the enemies of Zion would be made His footstool. Peter concluded the second point of his sermon in Acts 2:34-36: *"For David is not ascended into the heavens: but he saith himself, The Lord said unto my Lord, Sit thou on my right hand, Until I make thy foes thy footstool. Therefore let all the house of Israel know assuredly, that God hath made this same Jesus, whom ye have crucified, both Lord and Christ."* Peter here is still preaching to the House of Israel--no Gentiles. This second sign, like the first sign, concerned only Israel, mainly the exalted Christ who would deliver the House of Israel from those who oppressed it, at this time the Roman Empire.

What did this congregation of Israelites do when Peter completed his revelation of these two important messianic covenant signs that were fulfilled in the death and resurrection of Jesus Christ? Luke informs us that they were pricked in their heart and they said unto Peter and the rest of the apostles, the other eleven, *"What shall we do now that we have crucified the Messiah?"*

Let us read carefully what Peter told them to do. *"...Repent, and be baptized every one of you in the name of Jesus Christ for the remission of sins, and ye shall receive the gift of the Holy Ghost. For the promise is unto you, and to your children, and to all that are afar off, even as many as the Lord our God shall call"* (Acts 2:38-39). This particular scripture is another one that has further divided and separated from fellowship many believers in Christ--not because of the truth in the scripture, but rather because of what men have tried to interpret from it. It is difficult for me to understand why Christians would misunderstand it or misapply it. The Word is emphatic. Peter is replying to a question asked him by those who belonged to the House of Israel; there was not a Gentile among them. The answer Peter gave was to inform them what Israel must do to make restitution for crucifying their Messiah, the Lord Jesus Christ. Not only did it pertain to those Israelites in the land, but to those groups from eighteen nations that had come to Jerusalem on the day of Pentecost, and to all their brethren in these different lands. But nothing is said here about Gentiles, or is any reference to Gentiles even implied. In fact, Peter definitely excluded the Gentiles when he said, *"For the promise is unto you...."*

What Peter said here is of importance to us in knowing that Jesus was the promised Messiah who became our Savior on the cross. But the direct application of his message is for Israel only. What is the promise here that Peter is speaking of? The promise of the Kingdom, the covenant promise that when the Son of

David, the Holy One of Israel, reigned in Zion, He would take away the sins of His people and ungodliness from Jacob. This Israel-covenant truth is explained a thousand times over in the Old Testament, and why Christians cannot understand that this is the remission of sins that Peter was referring to is incomprehensible to me. This remission of sins that Peter talked about was through the visible administration of the Messiah; looking forward to the return of Christ in their lifetime.

The truth becomes doubly evident in the light of Peter's second sermon to Israel: *"The God of Abraham, and of Isaac, and of Jacob, the God of our fathers, hath glorified his Son Jesus; whom ye delivered up, and denied him in the presence of Pilate, when he was determined to let him go....But those things, which God had shewed by the mouth of all his prophets, that Christ should suffer, he hath so fulfilled. Repent ye therefore, and be converted, that your sins may be blotted out, when the times of refreshing shall come from the presence of the Lord; And he shall send Jesus Christ, which before was preached unto you"* (Acts 3:13,18-20).

The repentance, conversion, and baptism preached to Israel by Peter looked forward to the times of refreshing--the glorious Millennium, the Kingdom age--after God had sent Jesus Christ back to Israel. This was not according to faith, but according to the visible fulfilling of covenant signs. Peter here is preaching essentially what John the Baptist preached and what Jesus preached when the Kingdom was being offered. The only difference is that Peter preached, *"If you will repent, be converted* [meaning turn from your wicked ways], *and be baptized unto the remission of sins, then God will send that same Jesus whom you crucified back to be your Messiah and King. And when this happens, the times of refreshing will come in, the Kingdom from Heaven will be a reality, and from the presence of the Lord in Israel there shall come righteousness and your sins shall be taken away."*

Peter continued to inform Israel that when this glorious promise became a reality, then the children of the Kingdom, Israel, would take this gospel of the Kingdom into all the world and through Israel all nations would be blessed. *"Ye are the children of the prophets, and of the covenant which God made with our fathers, saying unto Abraham, And in thy seed shall all the kindreds of the earth be blessed"* (Acts 3:25).

I know there are churches today that practice and believe in water baptism according to Acts 2:38. They say it is the water baptism that takes away the sins, but even Peter didn't preach this. The baptism which Peter preached to Israel was in looking forward to remission of sins in the Kingdom. But these churches that teach water baptism for the remission of sins contend that they are the only New Testament church. And to the members of these churches, I would remind you in the kindest spirit of Christian love that you do not belong to a New Testament church at all. Your church is a covenant church according to the promise of God to the fathers of Israel. Of Peter's two sermons in the second and third chapters of Acts, the apostle himself said, *"...these things which I preach are according to the promises of the covenants."*

To whom are these promises of God made? To the Gentiles? Certainly not! *"Who are Israelites; to whom pertaineth the adoption, and the glory, and the covenants, and the giving of the law, and the service of God, and the promises"* ·(Rom. 9:4).

According to Paul's gospel, the gospel of grace, the hope we Gentiles have is not according to water baptism, not according to covenants or any promise of the Kingdom made to Israel, but only by faith in Jesus Christ and His shed blood, for He died for our sins.

"...God, who is rich in mercy, for his great love wherewith he loved us, Even when we were dead in sins hath quickened us together with Christ, (by grace ye are saved); And hath raised us up together, and made us sit together in heavenly places in Christ Jesus: That in the ages to come he might shew the exceeding riches of his grace in his kindness toward us through Christ Jesus. For by grace are ye saved through faith; and that not of yourselves: it is the gift of God: Not of works, lest any man should boast....Wherefore remember, that ye being in time past Gentiles in the flesh, who are called Uncircumcision by that which is called the Circumcision in the flesh made by hands; That at that time ye were without Christ, being aliens from the commonwealth of Israel, and strangers from the covenants of promise, having no hope, and without God in the world: But now in Christ Jesus ye who sometimes were far off are made nigh by the blood of Christ" (Eph. 2:4-13).

Beloved, this is the story of our salvation. This is the gospel of grace that Jesus Christ gave to Paul to preach to the Gentiles. Our salvation came not by the covenants, promises, types, symbols, or diverse washings, but wholly according to the sovereign grace of God through faith in Jesus Christ who shed His blood for us; who died in our place on the cross. And because we accept this great truth and through faith believe in Jesus Christ as our Savior, Christ our Lord is going to quicken us, make us alive in resurrection glory, lift us up to sit together with Him in heavenly places, and in the ages of eternity He will shower us with exceeding riches. This is the story, beloved. This is the gospel of grace.

But instead of preaching this gospel, the churches have divided, contended, fought, killed each other, spent valuable energy arguing about such things as promises under the covenants, and about covenant-ordinances such as baptism. Every church has its own particular code of baptism and woe unto the person who dares question it. But this is nothing new. Christians argued about baptism in Paul's day and it split them up into groups then, just as it does now. What does the Scripture have to say on this?

"For it hath been declared unto me of you, my brethren, by them which are of the house of Chloe, that there are contentions among you. Now this I say, that every one of you saith, I am of Paul; and I of Apollos; and I of Cephas [Peter]; and I of Christ. Is Christ divided? was Paul crucified for you? or were ye baptized in the name of Paul? I thank God that I baptized none of you, but Crispus and Gaius; Lest any should say that I had baptized in mine own name. And I baptized also the household of Stephanas: besides, I know not whether I baptized any other. For Christ sent me not to baptize, but to preach the gospel: not with wisdom of words, lest the cross of Christ should be made of none effect. For the preaching of the cross is to them that perish foolishness; but unto us which are saved, it is the power of God" (1 Cor. 1:11-18).

Here, in essence, is what Paul wrote to the Christians at Corinth: "It has been called to my attention that you are arguing and bickering among yourselves over baptism. Some say your baptism is better because you were baptized by Apollos, or Cephas, or of me. I think God that I have baptized none of you, save two or three, for Christ sent me not to baptize, but to preach the gospel, the cross of Christ, which is the power of God unto salvation for you Gentiles."

Paul declared that the gospel which Christ gave to him was the power of God unto salvation, and in 1 Corinthians 1:17, he emphasizes that water baptism is not a part of that gospel. Paul regretted that he had baptized anyone, for it brought division to the church and detracted from the preaching of the Gospel. Paul admonishes the Christians to get on with the business at hand--preaching the gospel of grace--and forget their petty differences over baptisms. The Devil has used water baptism more than any other single thing to split churches and hinder the work of Christ among Christians.

What we have said on the subject of New Testament water baptism in no way is to be interpreted as negating the importance of it to local church membership, to the congregation, and to the individual Christian. However, water baptism is in no way related to the gospel of grace, which is the power of God unto salvation. The baptism of Christians should best be left in the authority of the pastor of each local assembly. For the purpose of church fellowship and unity, water baptism is simply an open affirmation to the congregation and the world of an inward faith in Jesus Christ as Savior and Lord.

"Know ye not, that so many of us as were baptized into Jesus Christ were baptized into his death? Therefore we are buried with him by baptism unto death: that like as Christ was raised up from the dead by the glory of the Father, even so we also should walk in newness of life. For if we have been planted together in the likeness of his death, we shall be also in the likeness of his resurrection" (Rom. 6:3-5).

It may be debated both pro and con whether water baptism is the subject of the preceding scripture; but regardless, the gospel of grace committed to Paul to be preached to the Gentiles makes water baptism a sign of an inward faith in the atoning death of Jesus Christ and His resurrection, and nothing more. The sign on the front of your church may read: The First Baptist Church, The First Methodist Church, St. Joseph's Catholic Church, or some other title. However, the sign is for identification purposes only. It is what's on the inside that counts.

Chapter Seven

Entities of the Kingdom Gospel

Most Christians understand that during this dispensation, the gospel of grace is the message of God for the world. It is within the scope of this Divine revelation that Gentiles, who were without hope, promise, or covenant, come to God by faith in His Son, the Lord Jesus Christ, who died for the sins of the whole world. If Peter and the apostles to the Circumcision did not preach the gospel of grace, then why should we as Gentile believers attempt to appropriate that which they preached to Israel for ourselves? The answer should be obvious: let Israel have what God has given to them, and let us claim what God has given to us. This is not to detract from Peter's greatness in the sight of God, or to minimize his outstanding ministry. But rather, to help you understand what the Lord gave to Peter apart from what He committed to Paul.

Besides the fact that the messages Peter preached to Israel were evidently the gospel of the Kingdom, from the basic presentation of Christ according to the covenants, we can also know it was the gospel of the Kingdom because of the great number of Kingdom entities.

The most obvious of these additional signs that Peter did not preach the grace of God is that, until the conversion of Paul, grace is not mentioned in the book of Acts. Not once in Acts did Peter associate the grace of

God with his ministry. When Paul began to preach to the Gentiles, Paul talked about nothing else. We find the grace of God associated with Paul's message more than one hundred times.

But some will ask: What about the time when Peter came to the defense of Paul's gospel in Acts 15:11? *"But we* [Israel] *believe that through the grace of the Lord Jesus Christ we shall be saved even as they* [meaning Gentiles]...." Does this mean that Peter changed from the gospel of the Kingdom to preaching the gospel of grace according to our understanding after Acts 15? No, it certainly does not, for even Peter's understanding of the grace of God toward Israel was different from Paul's revelation of the grace of God toward the Gentiles. Even in the face of the growing hardness of heart of the Jews, and the overwhelming rejection by them of the offer of the Kingdom, basically Peter never changed his message. He continued to preach the return of the Messiah in that generation to take away the sins of Israel at His coming. Even though Israel had crucified their Messiah, through the grace of God they were given another chance. If they would repent, turn from their sins, and recognize that Jesus whom they crucified was the promised Holy One of Israel, then He would come back to bring in the Kingdom in accordance with His promise in Matthew 23:39: *"For I say unto you, Ye shall not see me henceforth, till ye shall say, Blessed is he that cometh in the name of the Lord."*

This was the grace of God that Peter referred to in Acts 15, and it was the message he continued to expound. For example, I refer you to Peter's epistle, which was written to the Israelites scattered abroad in A.D. 63, and I quote 1 Peter 1:13: *"Wherefore gird up the loins of your mind, be sober, and hope to the end for the grace that is to be brought unto you at the revelation of Jesus Christ."*

The revelation of Jesus Christ, as referred to by Peter, means, of course, His second coming.

We read of the results of Peter's first sermon to Israel in Acts 2:41: *"Then they that gladly received his word were baptized; and the same day there were added unto them about three thousand souls."* And we read of the fruit of the second sermon in Acts 4:4: *"Howbeit many of them which heard the word believed; and the number of the men was about five thousand."*

Numbering is a peculiarity of the Kingdom, but it is alien to the gospel of grace. Nowhere does Paul number Gentile conversions, nor does he even refer to church numbers in his epistles. Members of the Kingdom will be numbered, for conversion by the gospel of the Kingdom is a visible and tangible thing. However, only God can know whether a sinner saved by grace has received Christ as Savior and been born again into the body of Christ.

Next, we see the distinct difference between the ministry of Peter and the ministry of Paul in the meaning of *discipleship*. In the original Greek text of our New Testament, a *disciple* meant literally a follower or scholar of a particular person, or a student of a particular science, philosophy, or theology. The followers of Jesus Christ are called disciples in the four gospels because they were learning of Him and His Kingdom. Even the apostles were continually asking Jesus questions about the Kingdom of Heaven. Likewise, the members of the early Jewish Pentecostal church were called disciples. They were pointed by Peter to Christ as He would reign in the Kingdom, according to the covenants. In this sense, they were disciples, or continued to be learners of Christ and the Kingdom of Heaven. Under the ministry of Paul, only Jewish believers, or those who had been baptized with the baptism of John, continued to be called disciples. The word *disciple* in the New Testament fades out in Acts 21:16. Paul never referred to a Gentile believer in Christ--that is, a Gentile saved by the gospel of grace--as a disciple. The Gentile believers at Antioch saved under Paul's ministry were called Christians. A Christian is one who belongs to Christ and is indwelt by Christ, or one who is secure in Christ. If you lived in Tulsa, you would be called a Tulsan, and Paul says of the Christian's relation to Christ in Acts 17:28, *"For in him we live, and move, and have our being...."*

In all things connected with Peter's ministry we see the fulfilling of Old Testament prophecies relating to the Messiah and the Kingdom from Heaven. For example, we read this Kingdom promise to Israel in Isaiah 35:5-6: *"Then the eyes of the blind shall be opened, and the ears of the deaf shall be unstopped. Then shall the lame man leap as an hart, and the tongue of the dumb sing...."* Notice how completely this prophecy was fulfilled by Peter as a sign to Israel as he commanded the lame man to rise and walk in Acts 3:8: *"And he leaping up stood, and walked, and entered with them into the temple, walking, and leaping, and praising God."*

And many of the sick and afflicted came to Peter to be healed as he preached in Solomon's porch by the Temple--eyes of the blind were opened, the deaf heard, the mute spoke, and all manners of disease were healed, when even the shadow of Peter passed over the afflicted. But once again we notice how closely the ministry of Peter and the activities of the Jerusalem church centered around the Temple. Even the lame man followed Peter and John into the Temple. We read in the twenty-first chapter of Acts that the Jerusalem church even continued to offer sacrifices in the Temple and to observe the ordinances of the law for purification. Surely, this in itself should be sufficient proof that the Jerusalem church under the primacy of Peter was a covenant body working for repentance in Israel so that God would send Jesus back to bring in the Kingdom. The only authority extended to Peter, or any of the apostles and disciples at Jerusalem, over the Gentiles was according to covenant relationship of Jew and Gentile; and not according to the gospel of grace in which Jew and Gentile are alike. As Israel more and more turned from the gospel of the Kingdom preached by Peter, Jesus Christ gave Paul the message He wanted preached to the Gentiles; and thereafter, the ministry of the Jerusalem church to Gentiles declined and finally ceased altogether.

When Peter went down to Antioch and tried to correct the Gentile Christians about those things pertaining to eating under the law, Paul said of this event, *"But when Peter was come to Antioch, I withstood him to the face, because he was to be blamed"* (Gal. 2:11).

Peter had no authority under the commission given to Paul by Jesus Christ--the gospel of grace that was to be preached to the Gentiles. There is no evidence that Peter ever claimed or desired any authority over, or voice in, the Gentiles churches after the Antioch episode. God had made it plain that his ministry to Israel and Paul's ministry to the Gentiles were separate. Peter's ministry revolved around the Jewish Temple and it ended with the destruction of the Temple. The message which he preached to Israel will be resumed during the Tribulation period. There is no evidence that any of the Gentile churches established by Paul looked to Peter for leadership, or recognized him in any church leadership capacity whatsoever. Any claim for Peter's primacy over the Gentile church must be considered in light of Paul's declaration in Galatians 2:14: *"...I said unto Peter before them all, If thou, being a Jew, livest after the manner of Gentiles, and not as do the Jews, why compellest thou the Gentiles to live as do the Jews?"*

It is unscriptural to conclude that Peter established any kind of an appointive or elective office over the Gentile church age, yet over half of Christendom today still considers Peter the first universal church primate and they continue to perpetuate his office. This is just another one of the many church errors that have occurred because Christians have not rightly divided the Word and distinguished between the gospel of the Circumcision given to Peter and the gospel of the Uncircumcision given to Paul.

John the Baptist was a great man used mightily of God. He was given a powerful message in his day for Israel: *"Repent, for the kingdom of heaven is at hand."* But John the Baptist said that he and his message would decrease, while Jesus Christ and His message would increase. Peter was another great man of God, and he was given a powerful message to Israel. But the message that Peter preached to the Gentiles decreased. Peter wrote two epistles that are included in the twenty-seven books of the New Testament. Paul wrote fourteen of the New Testament books. Certainly, the two epistles of Peter are profitable to our understanding and edification just as all the books of the Bible are. However, the letters of Paul written to the Gentiles constitute our own direct mail from God. Failure to discern this peculiar truth, especially as set forth in the first fifteen chapters of Acts is why there are so many churches.

Chapter Eight

The Last Days of Peter

Once again we emphasize that in this study we are not attempting to detract from the ministry of Peter. Perhaps no man in God's service was ever given a more difficult and heart-rending mission. To know that his Lord had risen and was seated at the right hand of the Father, and to realize that God would send Jesus back upon evidence of repentance in Israel and an acceptance of Christ as Messiah, and yet see the Jews continue to harden their hearts must have been a terribly sad experience for this great apostle.

We know that Peter was definitely in Jerusalem in A.D. 50 when Paul went up to the Jerusalem church to explain that gospel which he preached among the Gentiles. There is some difference of opinion as to whether Peter or James was recognized as the head of the Jerusalem assembly at that time, but we note in Acts 15:7 that Peter spoke before James did. Therefore, it would appear that Peter was still recognized as the leader.

No mention is made of Peter by Luke in the twenty-first chapter of Acts when Paul turned from the leading of the Holy Spirit and went again to Jerusalem. Acts 21:18 informs us that Paul went into the house of James and all the elders of the Jerusalem church were present. This does not mean that James had replaced Peter as the head of the Jerusalem church, for it was common to vary the meeting places. All the elders were present so we must presume that Peter was among them. It appears though that when Peter wrote his first epistle in A.D. 63, about five years later, he was at Babylon.

It is evident from the twenty-first chapter of Acts that the ministry of Peter and the Jerusalem church continued to be centered about the Temple, and it was still considered by them to be the House of God. To the average Christian layman, this fact may not mean a great deal. However, to Bible teachers, pastors, ministers, and evangelists, it should be of paramount importance. The Sanhedrin and the Judaic priesthood tolerated the presence of the elders of the Jerusalem church in the Temple because James, Peter, and the other Jewish church elders continued to observe the ordinances of the Mosaic law. Regardless of how many times we read it, this is the only possible conclusion from Acts 21. The Jewish religious leaders continued to permit the Jerusalem church leaders to use the Temple for worship purposes; however, they considered Paul a blasphemer because he preached a different gospel to the Gentiles, one divorced from the Levitical rules and rituals. These facts are important to those who have the responsibility of instructing Christians how to rightly divide the Word.

As I have already observed, in A.D. 63, Peter was still preaching the basic doctrines of the gospel of the Kingdom to Israel. As long as the Temple was standing in Jerusalem, Peter was obligated under the commission of his gospel to continue to preach repentance to Israel, and to turn the Jews toward the truth that they had crucified their Messiah who was promised in the covenants. If they would believe in Christ and cry out to God to send Him back, David's greater Son would come back in like manner as He had promised and would bring first upon Israel and then the whole world the times of refreshing, the glorious Kingdom from Heaven. Paul preached the gospel of grace to the Gentiles, salvation by faith alone in Christ who died for the sins of the whole world. Paul told the Gentiles that salvation was apart from the Temple; that it was as close to them as their heart and their mouth (Rom. 10:8-10). But Peter informed the Jewish believers scattered abroad in A.D. 63 that the revelation of Jesus who would bring in the Kingdom was still their chief hope.

But even though Peter was obligated and bound to this mission of making a legal offer of the Kingdom to Israel, in his first epistle we begin to see evidence that the Holy Spirit was leading him to an understanding that this was not to be during that generation. The Roman Empire continued to strengthen its hold over Israel and was exerting pressure to bring Israel into the empire as a full supporting and cooperating ally. Rome offered all its conquered peoples the glorious opportunity to join the march of the Eternal City and share in the glory of her destiny. However, to those who refused and resisted only merciless annihilation awaited. This was what made Rome so strong and powerful, and in its basic political philosophy it was much like communism.

At the time Peter wrote his first epistle, a rebellious spirit against Roman oppression was growing in Israel. In A.D. 63, Flavius Josephus was the governor of Galilee, and he wrote of conditions in Israel at that time in his history of the Jews. Although Peter still held out hope that Christ, as prophesied by Malachi, would return to the Temple in his day and bring in the Kingdom, he gave evidence of knowing that the terrible judgment prophesied by Jesus Christ in the Temple Discourse against Israel was near at hand, and the destruction of the Temple, which the Lord told Peter personally would come about, was very near. Peter wrote to the disciples scattered about as recorded in 1 Peter 4:17: *"For the time is come that judgment must begin at the house of God: and if it first begin at us, what shall the end be of them that obey not the gospel of God?"*

The common interpretation of this scripture is that Peter was talking about the church, but obviously he was referring to the Temple. He was writing to the Jewish believers abroad about something that was imminent at that very time, and the Jerusalem church continued to look upon the Temple as the House of God, as indeed it was, according to the gospel of the Kingdom. And even as Peter still held forth the hope of the Kingdom, he seemed to have been attempting to condition the disciples abroad that the Kingdom offer would soon be set aside and to open the door for a reception of Paul's gospel, even to the household of faith in Israel. Declarations such as these were totally absent from Peter's earlier messages to Israel.

"And if ye call on the Father, who without respect of persons judgeth according to every man's work, pass the time of your sojourning here in fear: Forasmuch as ye know that ye were not redeemed with corruptible things, as silver and gold, from your vain conversation received by tradition from your fathers; But with the precious blood of Christ, as of a lamb without blemish and without spot" (1 Pet. 1:17-19).

"For all flesh is as grass, and all the glory of man as the flower of grass. The grass withereth, and the flower thereof falleth away: But the word of the Lord endureth for ever..." (1 Pet. 1:24-25).

"For Christ also hath once suffered for sins, the just for the unjust, that he might bring us to God, being put to death in the flesh, but quickened by the Spirit" (1 Pet. 3:18).

Peter wrote his second epistle at least three years after his first one. By this time, the Jewish revolt was already beginning in remote provincial areas. The woes pronounced upon Israel by Jesus in the Temple Discourse, and the destruction of the Temple and the dispersion of Israel into all nations prophesied in the Olivet Discourse, were nigh at hand. Peter knew he was going to die. Christ told him, as recorded in John 21:18-19 that he would die with his arms outstretched, signifying crucifixion, after he had been forced to abandon the site of his ministry in Jerusalem. Peter was to be killed by the Romans, for this was Rome's official method of execution. When Peter wrote his second epistle, he may have already been under house arrest, as we read in 2 Peter 1:14, *"Knowing that shortly I must put off this my tabernacle, even as our Lord Jesus Christ hath shewed me."*

While in Peter's second epistle we continue to find clear evidence of the Kingdom message, he endeavors to reconcile his gospel with that gospel preached by Paul to the Gentiles. Instead of addressing his second epistle to a select group of Israelites, he writes simply to *"...them that have obtained like precious faith with us through the righteousness of God and our Saviour Jesus Christ"* (2 Pet. 1:1). He makes no difference between Jews and Gentiles as he did three years earlier (1 Pet. 2:12), and he speaks of the second coming of Christ as a distant reality rather than a present hope. And in his second epistle, Peter speaks more freely about the grace of God. The fact that the leader of the Jerusalem church had put his stamp of approval upon the gospel of Paul as he closes his ministry signified that he accepted the evident truth that the Kingdom would be shortly set aside, and the only hope for Israel thereafter, until the end of the age, would be in the gospel of grace which Paul preached.

"Wherefore, beloved, seeing that ye look for such things, be diligent that ye may be found of him in peace, without spot,

and blameless. And account that the long-suffering of our Lord is salvation; even as our beloved brother Paul also according to the wisdom given unto him hath written unto you; As also in all his epistles, speaking in them of these things; in which are some things hard to be understood, which they that are unlearned and unstable wrest, as they do also the other scriptures, unto their own destruction" (2 Pet. 3:14-16).

In these last recorded words of Peter in the Bible, he seemed to be urging everyone, including the Jewish believers, to heed the epistles of Paul, and even though hard to understand according to the covenants of Israel, to deny the revelation given to Paul would mean their own destruction. Peter's reference to Paul writing to them is added evidence that Paul wrote Hebrews.

Chapter Nine

Times of the Gentiles

As we have already pointed out, when Peter wrote his second epistle, he knew that he was soon to be crucified. Most Bible footnotes place the writing of the second epistle in the year A.D. 66; however, Fausset states that the date is more likely A.D. 69. If the year was A.D. 66, then Peter was probably charged before the Roman court by the Sanhedrin and the Jewish priesthood, and tried in much the same manner as Jesus was. If his second epistle was written in A.D. 69, then his crucifixion would have been a direct result of the Roman siege of Jerusalem, which began in A.D. 68.

When the Roman army began to entrench itself about Jerusalem in preparation for the siege, many of the disciples of the Jerusalem church fled, for they knew according to judgments pronounced by Jesus upon that generation, the city, and the Temple, were near fulfillment. Ancient records indicate that some of the disciples made good their escape while others were caught and crucified. The Lord prophesied that Peter would be forcibly taken from his mission post and then crucifixion would follow. Whether Peter was taken by the disciples against his will out of the city and later caught by Roman soldiers and crucified, or whether he was arrested first, imprisoned, and then taken outside the city to be executed, is a matter of speculation and needs no further comment. However, we can be certain that

Peter did meet death by crucifixion, carried out upon orders of Roman authority, somewhere between A.D. 66 and A.D. 69.

Some contend that tradition, and even some scriptures, indicates that Peter left Jerusalem and went to Rome in about A.D. 60, and even pastored a church there. However, I find no evidence of this in the New Testament. Neither does Paul in any of his prison epistles mention that Peter was in Rome. It is evident that Paul received visitors and was kept well informed as to all news relative to the churches, and especially the Christians in Rome. Had Peter been in Rome at any time between A.D. 61 and A.D. 66, Paul would have been sure to mention it. Peter, in his first epistle, indicates he went to Babylon where there was still a large Jewish population, but by A.D. 66 he probably had returned to Jerusalem. It is clear from the history of Josephus that during this period, Israel more and more prayed in the Temple for the Messiah to come and deliver them from bondage and bring His glory upon the land. Peter was bound to continue to preach that if Israel would repent, recognize the fact that they had crucified their Messiah, and cry out for God to send Him back, He would return.

We read in the account of the siege of Jerusalem, as described by Josephus, that that condemned generation was given every Kingdom age sign possible. During the siege, three emperors of Rome were killed and the crown finally fell upon the head of Vespasian, so that his son, Titus, would be a prince before the final assault came, in accordance with Daniel's prophecy. Before the city fell, a man whom no one had ever seen wandered through the city pronouncing three woes. The famine became so great that babies were taken away from their mothers to be eaten. This was in accordance with Old Testament prophecies and a like prophecy given by Jesus in the Olivet Discourse. In addition, according to Josephus, strange ships appeared over Jerusalem in the skies in fierce conflict. The noise was so great that it was even heard in the streets of Jerusalem. The only thing that kept up the courage and determination of the Jews during the latter days of the siege was the hope that the Messiah would yet come to the Temple and save them. Josephus wrote that the priests even spread false rumors that the Messiah was seen coming toward Jerusalem to keep up the spirits of the people.

Perhaps there was never a better trained and disciplined army in the history of the world than the Roman army. When it became evident that Jewish resistance inside Jerusalem was crumbling and the walls were breached, Titus issued strict orders that the Temple was not to be damaged in any way, for it was considered by him to be the most magnificent structure in all the world. All Romans had a deep appreciation for art and architecture. But, according to the prophecy of Jesus, the Temple had to be destroyed, and Josephus informs us that it was through Divine intervention that Titus' orders were disobeyed and the Temple burned. Quoting the historian:

> "...One of the soldiers, without staying for any orders, and without any concern or dread upon him at so great an undertaking, and being hurried on by a certain divine fury, snatched somewhat out of the materials that were on fire, and being lifted up by another soldier, he set fire to a golden window...."

As the Temple was burning, the priests rushed to put out the fire, for if the Temple burned, all hope of deliverance through the Messiah was gone. Josephus informs us that the Roman soldiers cut their throats as they caught them and the blood ran from the altar out of the building. There were members of the priesthood who could not get to the Temple to defend it; and they pleaded with Titus to spare their lives. However, Titus informed them that inasmuch as they no longer had a Temple, there was no further need for them. He ordered them killed to the last one. In one day, the Temple was destroyed, the entire priesthood killed, and Jerusalem fell to the invading Roman army. The carrying out of God's judgments against Israel for the rejection of their Messiah had indeed begun at the House of God and it has endured now for almost two thousand years.

We read in 1 Samuel 4:21 that when the ark departed from Israel, it was a sign that the glory of the Lord had departed and God had forsaken His people. Through the ministry of Peter and the Jerusalem church, with subsequent signs given during the siege of Jerusalem by Titus, God had fulfilled every legal obligation to that generation. When the Temple burned, the offer of the Kingdom officially terminated. The Temple had to be destroyed in order for the dispensation of grace to come in all its fullness.

The pivot of the prophecies concerning Israel, as outlined in the Olivet Discourse, was the destruction of the Temple. *"And they [Israel] shall fall by the edge of the sword, and shall be led away captive into all nations: and Jerusalem shall be trodden down of the Gentiles, until the times of the Gentiles be fulfilled"* (Luke 21:24). This is the only scripture in the Bible where the "times of the Gentiles" is mentioned. The "times of the Gentiles" as spoken of by Jesus is predicated upon the absence of Israel from the land and the possession of Jerusalem by Gentile authority. It appears to me from a close study of the Scriptures that these "times" in which God would deal with Gentile nations began when He stopped dealing with Israel as a nation. The ascendancy of Gentile authority over Israel began with Babylon, but God did not withdraw or terminate the offer of the Kingdom until the Temple was destroyed in A.D. 70, I believe, in accordance with Luke 21:24, that the "times of the Gentiles" began with the destruction of the Temple, and ended June 6, 1967 when Israel formally annexed the old city of Jerusalem.

The "times of the Gentiles" is not the same as the dispensation of grace, but approximates it. The ascendancy of Gentile power over Israel began with Babylon and will end at Armageddon. The Gentile church age (Gentile in the sense that Paul said it would be the Gentiles who would hear and believe) began with the Pauline epistles and will end at the Rapture.

How has God dealt with the Gentile nations during the "times of the Gentiles"? He has blessed them in accordance with their adherence to His order for human government, and in accordance also with Paul's declaration in 1 Timothy 2:1-4: *"I exhort therefore, that, first of all, supplications, prayers, intercessions, and giving of thanks, be made for all men; For kings, and for all that are in authority; that we may lead a quiet and peaceable life in all godliness and honesty. For this is good and acceptable in the sight of God our Saviour; Who will have all men to be saved, and to come unto the knowledge of the truth."*

All you have to do to understand why God has so blessed our nation is to study carefully the Declaration of Independence in light of this scripture. During the "times of the Gentiles," nations have determined their own destiny in accordance with their faithfulness to God's will for this age in a national sense--to provide freedom of ideas, will, and mobility for men so that they might have every opportunity to come to the knowledge of the truth that Jesus Christ is the Savior of the world. Nations have risen and fallen. For example, Spain grew into a great power, but it declined when it took up the sword in the Name of Christ to conquer the world. England grew to a world power through the spirit of a great revival and dedication to law, order, and the freedom of men. It declined when it abused that authority and has further declined under socialism.

But we must also remember that freedom of national destiny during the "times of the Gentiles" was limited to those centuries in which Israel was no longer in view. Israel again came into view at the end of World War I with the signing of the Balfour Declaration. Russia fell to communism in accordance with Ezekiel 38 and 39, and since World War I, world conditions on the national level have developed according to the foreknowledge of God, growing worse and worse--heading toward Armageddon.

If Christians understand these basic truths, they have no difficulty discerning which is the correct doctrine concerning the second coming of Christ--premillennialism, post-millennialism, or A-millennialism. These are three basic doctrines that have further divided and separated those who name the Name of Christ.

Peter, as he was assured that his execution was near and realized the Kingdom would be set aside for another age with the approaching destruction of Jerusalem, pointed to the return of Christ as the promise and consummation of His Gospel, and he turned with his last words and pointed to the epistles of Paul as evidently containing the message of the Lord's salvation until this Kingdom be brought in. Peter extended his gospel over, or beyond, an entire age.

Paul, in his last epistle, 2 Timothy, as he realized the time for his execution had come, found no reason to turn over his ministry to another, but rather, offered the revelation that the Lord had given him as the salvation for the Gentiles. In 2 Timothy 4:17, Paul indicates that his life was spared for a time so that the Gentiles might have the complete revelation concerning the mystery of the church, and we find the completed gospel of grace and revelation that was hidden from all former ages, revealed in the prison epistles. In his epistles, Paul did not point to the literal return of Christ to Israel as the hope of the church and the consummation of His Gospel, but rather to our gathering together to meet the Lord in the air. We refer to this as the Rapture of the church.

Post-millennialists continue to work to bring in a kingdom on earth. Today, their efforts are magnified through the ecumenical movement. The A-millennialists see no significance in the refounding of Israel as a nation, or the fulfillment of the end-time prophecies that are now occurring almost on a daily basis. They see the return of Christ as an ambiguous and distant possibility, and then only to destroy the world. To them, the idea that Christ will return to establish a Kingdom from Heaven here on earth, in accordance with the covenants that God made with Israel, and in accordance with the gospel preached by Peter, is utter nonsense. But these divisions among those who name the Name of Christ, concerning post-millennialism, A-millennialism, and pre-millennialism have arisen because many have not been able to discern that in the gospel of the Kingdom, as preached by Peter, there are still promises to Israel; and in the gospel of grace, as preached by Paul, we find God's promise to the Gentiles.

Chapter Ten

The Conversion of Paul

Jesus Christ had commanded that the Gospel be preached to all the world, beginning at Jerusalem. This was the mission which He gave to the early Pentecostal assembly under the leadership of Peter. Peter preached the first sermons of this Gospel to Israel. As we have already brought out, it was the gospel of the Kingdom. According to the covenants, the Messiah was to be a light to the Gentiles through Israel. The Holy Spirit, with much prodding again showed Peter that he must take this Gospel to the Gentiles. Some contend that Peter preached the gospel of grace to the household of Cornelius, but we must remember that the apostles at Jerusalem knew nothing of the gospel that Paul preached until the fifteenth chapter of Acts.

Cornelius was a devout Gentile. According to the Word, he was a Jewish proselyte. He knew of the covenants, and therefore, he believed the Gospel which Peter preached to him. We continue the development of the ministry of the Jerusalem church in the eighth chapter of Acts and read that the disciples were scattered abroad. Phillip went down into Samaria and preached the Gospel, but we must keep in mind that he was acting under the authority of Peter and still preached essentially the same gospel that Peter preached, which was the gospel of the Circumcision. We know from the ministry of Jesus in Samaria that even though the

Samaritans were of mixed Gentile blood, they still knew of the promises that God had made to the fathers. We read that as the disciples went abroad preaching the Word, they healed the sick and performed many miracles as signs of the Kingdom (Acts 8:4-8). We read also that those who believed and received the Word were baptized. However, these were still converts of the Kingdom promise; they had heard Jesus preached according to the covenants made to Israel. At that time, this was the only Gospel these Jewish disciples of the Jerusalem church had to preach.

The Levitical priesthood in charge of the Temple worship in Jerusalem still, for the most part, had a strong grip on the masses in Israel. The stoning of Stephen with his stirring revelation to Israel (*"I see the heavens opened, and the Son of man standing on the right hand of God"*) made no impression on the priesthood or the Pharisees. God kept the offer of the Kingdom open to Israel through the testimony of the apostles and the Jerusalem assembly, for this was a legal covenant obligation as long as the Temple was standing. And even after the last two surviving apostles had left (Peter and John--Peter crucified and John exiled to the salt mines of Patmos), God kept the Kingdom promise open through many signs, as related by Josephus, even as the Temple crumbled to the ground and the ashes of the timbers cooled, the doors to the Kingdom closed. They would not be opened until a refounded nation of Israel, regathered out of all nations, would say of Jesus, *"...Blessed is he that cometh in the name of the Lord"* (Matt. 23:39).

And so, as one age closed, God opened a new dispensation to the world, or as Paul explained in Romans 11:25, *"...blindness in part is happened to Israel, until the fulness of the Gentiles be come in."*

According to God's foreknowledge that Israel would reject the gospel of the Kingdom and His everlasting will that not any should perish, He began the new age to the Gentiles even while Israel was yet dying. The man he chose to be the first apostle, preacher, and proclaimer of the new dispensation was the Apostle Paul, the apostle to the Gentiles. We must accept the inspiration of the Word and the infallibility of the Scriptures in Paul's declaration recorded in 1 Timothy 1:16: *"Howbeit for this cause I obtained mercy, that in me first Jesus Christ might shew forth all longsuffering, for a pattern to them which should hereafter believe on him to life everlasting."* Paul set forth the Gospel he preached as a new gospel, not given to him by Peter, the church at Jerusalem, or any man, but declared it came by a distinct and Divine revelation from Jesus Christ. Paul declared emphatically in Ephesians 3:1-3 that this revelation concerning the dispensation of grace was given to him first, not to Peter or the church at Jerusalem, but to him first, to take to the Gentiles.

The uniqueness and the complete separation of Paul's gospel of grace from the gospel of the Kingdom preached by Peter and the Jewish disciples was to be set forth in the manner of its presentation. The ministry of the Jerusalem Pentecostal assembly began with power from on high; they talked in other languages, though they were uneducated Galileans. They healed the sick and performed many miracles. But Paul showed no such miracles and signs to the Gentiles. Paul talked in other tongues, or languages, because he was a master of foreign languages. He was, without a doubt, the best educated man of his day. He was a brilliant lawyer, a student of Gamaliel, and a graduate of the Jerusalem law school. Both Scripture and tradition indicate that he could speak in seventeen languages or dialects. Acts

21:37-40, alone, brings out that he spoke fluent Egyptian, Greek, and Hebrew. He was a Pharisee by sect, and an avid student of the Old Testament Scriptures, history, Jewish tradition, and law. His associations in his home town of Tarsus brought him into contact with people from all the then-known world. While an Israelite of the tribe of Benjamin, he was also a citizen of Rome. The Word informs us that he was a young man at the time of the stoning of Stephen, yet the Scriptures indicate that he was a member of the Sanhedrin, of which membership was usually composed of the elderly sages of Israel. Paul would be classified as a genius in our day.

The Jewish disciples that preached the gospel of the Kingdom were especially prepared for their mission by the Holy Spirit on the day of Pentecost. God chose Paul for the mission to preach the gospel of grace. The message that Paul would preach to the Gentiles would not be according to covenants and signs, but by sovereign grace on God's part and simple faith on man's part. Paul was wonderfully equipped. This truth is brought out in the Lord's instructions to Ananias in Acts 9:15: *"But the Lord said unto him, Go thy way: for he is a chosen vessel unto me, to bear my name before the Gentiles, and kings, and the children of Israel."*

Young Saul was, without a doubt, the most devout Jew in all Israel. In his epistles, he refers to himself as being before his conversion a Hebrew of Hebrews, a Pharisee and a son of a Pharisee, and a keeper of the commandments. Being a devout Jew demanded just as devout opposition to the Jerusalem church, and Saul was the most rabid prosecutor of the disciples. He was dedicated to the proposition of stamping out those who preached Jesus was the Christ. His conversion from an Orthodox Jew to a believer in Christ was just as unique as the Gospel that he was to preach. His meeting with the Lord on the road to Damascus is recorded in Acts 9:3-5: *"And as he journeyed, he came near Damascus: and suddenly there shined round about him a light from heaven: And he fell to the earth, and heard a voice saying unto him, Saul, Saul, why persecutest thou me? And he said, Who art thou, Lord? And the Lord said, I am Jesus whom thou persecutest...."*

Agnostics have ridiculed Paul's experience as a nervous breakdown, heat prostration, or sun stroke. However, Paul himself never doubted that he had truly seen the Lord. He referred to his meeting with the Lord face-to-face on the road to Damascus in 1 Corinthians 15:7-9: *"After that, he was seen of James; then of all the apostles. And last of all he was seen of me also, as of one born out of due time. For I am the least of the apostles, that am not meet to be called an apostle, because I persecuted the church of God."*

Paul associated the expression "born out of due time" with his seeing the Lord as related in the ninth chapter of Acts. This declaration of Paul also has an important relationship to our study of the difference between the gospel of the Circumcision and the gospel of the Uncircumcision. In being born (perhaps the correct interpretation would be "born anew" or "born into a new creation"), Paul put himself into a class by himself among the other apostles.

It has been brought out by many that Paul's conversion on the road to Damascus is a type of the conversion that will come to Israel at the second coming of Christ. His hardness of heart against the truth that Jesus was the Messiah was typical of the rejection of Israel to this truth. It took a visible confrontation with Jesus to make him realize that this One whom he despised and hated was truly the Christ. As he looked upon Jesus, he doubtless saw the nail prints in His hands, and Zechariah informs us that when the Lord comes back to Israel at the beginning of the Kingdom age, they will look upon the nail prints in His hands. The blindness that came over Paul is representative of the blindness that has been on Israel these many centuries. The blindness will be removed from Israel as the spirit of grace is poured out upon them, and the blindness from Paul's eyes came off as he received the Holy Spirit, as we read in Acts 9:17: *"...receive thy sight, and be filled with the Holy Ghost."* Paul said of his meeting with Jesus, *"...his grace...was bestowed upon me..."* (1 Cor. 15:10).

Now why would Paul refer to himself as an Israelite born out of due time? Paul realized that the rebirth of Israel, accompanied by the pouring out of the spirit of grace, whereby they would become the sons of God, would not come about until Jesus Christ returned to bring in the Kingdom. But the spirit of grace had already been bestowed upon him, and as he was born again of the Spirit he considered himself to have received this favor of God that is promised to Israel in Hosea 1:10 and many other Old Testament scriptures, ahead of time. *"Yet the number of the children of Israel shall be as the sand of the sea, which cannot be measured nor numbered; and it shall come to pass, that in the place where it was said unto them, Ye are not my people, there is shall be said unto them, Ye are the sons of the living God."* This is why Paul declared that he, being an Israelite, was as one born out of due time, the Greek meaning "born before his time." And this is also why Paul later declared that in this, he was the first to receive the grace of God, and he had become an example for all those who would by faith receive this gospel which he preached. His conversion was unique of all the twelve apostles and the disciples of the Jerusalem church; and the unique ministry which was given to Paul to preach to Israel, to kings, and to the Gentiles increased as the ministry of Peter and the Jerusalem church decreased.

The ministry of Paul was different in another way in that he was the first to be saved according to the sovereign grace of God. He was a Jew and as long as the promise of the Kingdom was in effect, he was also an heir to the Kingdom promises given in the covenants. As an Israelite, he had a legal obligation to declare Christ to Israel according to the covenants. While Paul, in nearly all his epistles, declared his calling to be an apostle to the Gentiles, we read of the first sermon he preached in Acts 9:20, *"And straightway he preached Christ in the synagogues, that he is the Son of God."* Thereafter, wherever Paul went he always went first into the synagogues to declare that Christ the Messiah had come. This was in accordance with the commandment given him by Jesus, that he was to declare the name of Christ before Israel and before the Gentiles. The order of his ministry was recorded in Romans 1:16: *"For I am not ashamed of the gospel of Christ: for it is the power of God unto salvation to every one that believeth; to the Jew first, and also to the Greek."*

However, we should keep in mind that Paul did not preach the same sermon to the Jews that he preached to the Gentiles. We read in Acts 16:3 that Paul's ministry to the Jews continued to be in the spirit of the gospel of the Kingdom; for if there had come about a national repentance in Israel, and Christ had come back at that time to bring in the Kingdom, these Jews would have been deprived of their rightful inheritance. When Paul returned to Jerusalem, as recorded in the twenty-first chapter of Acts, the brethren there falsely accused him of preaching the gospel of grace to the Jews: *"And they are informed of thee, that thou teachest all the Jews which are among the Gentiles to forsake Moses, saying that they ought not to circumcise their children, neither to walk after the customs. What is it therefore? the multitude must needs come together: for they will hear that thou art come"* (vss. 21-22).

Does this sound like the Jerusalem church and the Apostle Paul preached the same gospel? Paul was even bound by his citizenship in Israel to keep those Jews to whom he preached steadfast in the customs and traditions of Israel, including the Mosaic law. He declared Jesus to the Jews according to the covenants, and not according to the gospel of grace which he preached to the Gentiles. Of course, the final break with the gospel of the Kingdom came in Acts 28:28 where he declared to the delegation of Jews that had come to visit him in prison, *"Be it known therefore unto you, that the salvation of God is sent unto the Gentiles, and they will hear it."* It was after this that he wrote his prison epistles in which he revealed the complete mystery of the Gentile church age, the promises of God to Gentile believers, and the great inheritance awaiting those who make up the body of Christ.

Chapter Eleven

Faith or Works?

For the scriptural foundation of this chapter, let us return to the twenty-first chapter of Acts. It is my opinion that this particular chapter in Acts is the most neglected one in the New Testament. It is evident that as Israel turned away once again from the promise of the Kingdom through the Messiah, Paul's obligation to preach Jesus to the Jews according to the covenants was being set aside. The Lord was turning him more and more to the Gentiles with the gospel of grace. In spite of the Holy Spirit warning Paul three times in the twenty-first chapter of Acts that he was not to return to Jerusalem, we find the apostle to the Gentiles going back to the Jerusalem church and the Temple. To illustrate to James and all the brethren at the Jerusalem church that he was still observing the law of Moses and remaining steadfast in the promises of the covenants, Paul did as James and the elders of the church instructed him to do. He placed himself under the ceremony of the old Levitical law for purification, and we read in Acts 21:26 that at the end of the seven days a sacrifice was going to be offered in the Temple for Paul's sins. God intervened and stopped the proceedings before the sacrifice could be offered, but we notice the reason the Jews objected was because of the presence of Paul in the Temple. It would seem apparent that the Jerusalem church continued to observe the law of Moses and to offer sacrifices in the Temple for transgressions against the law even as late as A.D. 58. At this late date, the Jerusalem church evidently still taught that remission of sins would be accomplished when God sent Jesus back and Israel would be made righteous by His literal presence. For this reason, the elders of the Jerusalem church continued to observe the law and offer up animal sacrifices.

It is generally accepted that the Apostle John wrote his gospel and all of his epistles about twenty years after the Temple was destroyed. John wrote in chapter three, verse two of his first epistle, *"Beloved, now are we the sons of God, and it doth not yet appear what we shall be: but we know that, when he shall appear, we shall be like him; for we shall see him as he is."* For one of the twelve apostles to declare that *"...now we are the sons of God"* was a momentous declaration.

As Paul arrived at the house of James, he was met by the elders of the Jerusalem church, who greeted him with these words, *"...Thou seest, brother, how many thousands of Jews there are which believe; and they are all zealous of the law* [the law of Moses as declared in subsequent scriptures]" (Acts 21:20). Nothing could be more plain than that the assembly at Jerusalem was not only operating under the covenants, but were diligent to do the works commanded by the law which still pointed forward to the coming of Messiah (Gal. 3:24). Under the gospel of the Circumcision, which was committed to Peter, the keeping of the law was just as much an integral part as repentance and water baptism. It is a promise of the Kingdom that the law will go forth from Zion unto all nations, and as the Jerusalem brethren were yet operating under the gospel of the Kingdom in A.D. 58, James and the elders were encouraged by the fact that the members of the Jerusalem church kept the Mosaic law in all things.

When we discuss with those who hold to the point of view that a believer is not justified or saved by faith alone, invariably they will point with great emphasis to the epistle of James. The purpose of the epistle of James is to set forth the precept that a man is not justified by faith alone, but by works also, and unless the works of the new law are made manifest in the testimony and service of the believer, all his faith is vain, or counted for naught. *"Ye see then how that by works a man is justified, and not by faith only....For as the body without the spirit is dead, so faith without works is dead also"* (James 2:24,26).

But to what man or men was James referring? We don't have to speculate as to whom James addressed his epistle, for we read right away in James 1:1, *"James, a servant of God and of the Lord Jesus Christ, to the twelve tribes which are scattered abroad, greeting."* We read in the second chapter of this epistle that James wrote to those Israelites scattered abroad about the importance of keeping the law. James does not indicate in a single verse of his epistle that he was writing to Gentile believers. In fact, it would appear that James was the speaker in Acts 21:25, when he told Paul concerning the keeping of the law, *"As touching the Gentiles which believe, we have written and concluded that they observe no such thing...."* Even James and the elders of the church at Jerusalem recognized there was a difference between Paul's ministry to the Gentiles and Peter's ministry to Israel.

Paul is the only man in the Bible who claimed to be a God-appointed apostle to the Gentiles. Paul is the only man in the Bible who claimed to have received a revelation from Jesus Christ concerning the Gentile church age. Paul is the only man in the Bible who claimed to be an exclusive teacher for the Gentiles. Paul is the only one mentioned in the New Testament who claimed to have received the gospel from the Lord that was to be preached to the Gentiles. *"For there is one God, and one mediator between God and men, the man Christ Jesus; Who gave himself a ransom for all, to be testified in due time. Whereunto I am ordained a preacher, and an apostle, (I speak the truth in Christ, and lie not;) a teacher of the Gentiles in faith and verity"* (1 Tim. 2:5-7).

Paul declared that the truth that Jesus, the one mediator between God and man, had offered Himself as a ransom for all was to be testified or preached in due time. This truth was hidden from the apostles and disciples of the Jerusalem church. But in due time, or as Israel began to reject the gospel of the Kingdom, Paul was called to be an apostle to the Gentiles. He was ordained by Jesus Christ to be a preacher to the Gentiles, and that which Jesus Christ gave him to teach the Gentiles in faith was that Christ Jesus had given Himself as a ransom for all. Christ on the cross had redeemed men from the penalty of sin with His own precious blood, and this great salvation was available to all who would receive it by faith. In the order of events according to time, Paul was the first to preach this gospel. In testifying of his message and mission, Paul declared, *"...I speak the truth in Christ, and lie not...."*

As aliens to the covenants and commonwealth of Israel, we must believe that Paul spoke the truth, or else as Gentile believers we have no hope except through the witness of Israel in the world, and since national Israel has been cut off from God during the dispensation of grace, we would be of all men most miserable. Unless Paul spoke the truth, we are yet enemies of God and lost in sin.

Every one of Paul's epistles to the Gentiles is devoted to informing us that our salvation is according to sovereign grace and we are justified before God and saved from death unto eternal life by faith in Jesus Christ. This is the volume of God's truth for us. This is the good news that Paul preached to the Gentiles:

"Now to him that worketh is the reward not reckoned of grace, but of debt. But to him that worketh not, but believeth on him that justifieth the ungodly, his faith is counted for righteousness" (Rom. 4:4-5). **Justification by faith, not works.**

"Therefore being justified by faith, we have peace with God through our Lord Jesus Christ: By whom also we have access by faith into this grace wherein we stand, and rejoice in the hope of the glory of God" (Rom. 5:1-2). **We have peace with God through faith in Jesus Christ, not by works.**

"But the righteousness which is of faith speaketh on this wise....The word is nigh thee, even in thy mouth, and in thy heart: that is, the word of faith, which we preach; That if thou shalt confess with thy mouth the Lord Jesus, and shalt believe in thine heart that God hath raised him from the dead, thou shalt be saved" (Rom. 10:6-10). **Salvation by faith, not works.**

"If any man's works abide which he hath built thereupon, he shall receive a reward. If any man's works shall be burned, he shall suffer loss: but he himself shall be saved; yet so as by fire" (1 Cor. 3:14-15). **Christian labors earn a reward, but count for nothing concerning salvation.**

"But that no man is justified by the law in the sight of God, it is evident: for, The just shall live by faith" (Gal. 3:11). **The just, the righteous before God shall have everlasting life, not because of any works or any deed of the law, but because of their faith in Jesus Christ.**

"For by grace are ye saved through faith; and that not of yourselves: it is the gift of God: Not of works, lest any man should boast. For we are his workmanship, created in Christ Jesus unto good works, which God hath before ordained that we should walk in them" (Eph. 2:8-10). **Salvation to Gentiles is according to the grace of God; it is His gift to us. It**

is extended in grace and accepted through faith, not of works, or else it would not be a gift. We do not work to be saved; we work because we have been saved.

"...I have suffered the loss of all things, and do count them but dung, that I may win Christ, And be found in him, not having mine own righteousness, which is of the law, but that which is through the faith of Christ, the righteousness which is of God by faith: That I may know him, and the power of his resurrection...." (Phil. 3:8-10). We have the hope of resurrection glory, not because of our works or deeds according to the law, but because we believe that Christ died for our sins and that He was raised from the dead for our justification. Not works--just faith.

"...be thou partaker of the afflictions of the gospel according to the power of God; Who hath saved us, and called us with an holy calling, not according to our works, but according to his own purpose and grace, which was given us in Christ Jesus before the world began, But is now made manifest by the appearing of our Saviour Jesus Christ, who hath abolished death, and hath brought life and immortality to light through the gospel: Whereunto I am appointed a preacher, and an apostle, and a teacher of the Gentiles" (2 Tim. 1:8-11). God has saved us, and called us to a glorious inheritance purposed in Christ Jesus before the world began, not because of our works or anything that we have done; simply because we have believed, and received this gift of God by faith in the Son of God who died for our sins.

If salvation is by faith, how could it possibly be progressive? If our salvation depends not even one iota on ourselves, but on the finished work of Christ, how can one who has been saved ever be lost? I cannot find a single scripture in the Pauline epistles that indicates Paul ever doubted the assurance of his salvation or any scripture that indicates a child of God by faith in Jesus Christ would ever be lost.

The failure of Christians to understand whether they are saved by faith, by works, or by both, has resulted in a further division of Christendom into various churches, denominations, and sects. The reason for these differences on the doctrines of works and faith came about because theologians failed to separate the ministry of Paul and the gospel of grace he was given to preach from Peter and the Jerusalem assembly. This is just one more reason why we have so many churches.

Chapter Twelve

Mystery of the Church

In Paul's arrest at the Temple, as recorded in the twenty-first chapter of Acts, we see God turning the Apostles Paul more fully to the Gentiles. We read in the twenty-eighth chapter of Acts that when he arrived in Rome he first preached to the Jews concerning Jesus according to the law of Moses and the prophets. After the evidence he presented to the Jews that Jesus was the Messiah was again rejected, the Holy Spirit opened Paul's understanding that Israel's eyes were closed and their hearts hardened against the truth. God let Paul know that his obligation to preach Jesus to Israel according to the covenants had ended. Paul not had only one mission: to preach Christ to all men according to sovereign grace.

Although Paul's ministry to the Uncircumcision had been kept separate from Peter's ministry to the Circumcision, the Gentile believers were still bound by the terms of the Jerusalem council (Acts 15) to observe certain things that had a relation to the law. For example, it was brought out by the elders of the Jerusalem church in the twenty-first chapter of Acts that they were not to eat certain meats offensive to the Jews. However, when God spoke to Paul that his ministry to Israel had been fulfilled, Paul cut all ties of the Gentile church with the Jerusalem assembly completely and finally. We see evidence of this in the first epistle he wrote to the

Gentiles after he arrived at Rome: *"Let no man therefore judge you in meat, or in drink, or in respect of an holyday, or of the new moon, or of the sabbath days"* (Col. 2:16).

Because the Word has not been rightly divided and preached, there are certain groups and denominations today who contend we should observe these old agreements made at the Jerusalem council, and refrain from eating certain things, and also, worship only on the Sabbath, which is Saturday. The fact that Gentile believers are not bound by such Mosaic ordinances is so obvious that I am even reticent to mention it. Paul's instructions to Gentile believers after Acts 28:28 are to let no man judge, criticize, or condemn them in meat, drink, a holy day, or the Sabbath. I would have no basis for criticizing a church that wanted to meet only on those Fridays that fell on the thirteenth day of the month. And while an excess of pork is not good for bodily health, if a Christian wants to eat pork three times a day, three hundred and sixty-five days a year, I have no scriptural grounds to either forbid or criticize him. Because so many who name the Name of Christ today have not rightly distinguished between the ministry of Peter and the ministry of Paul, millions of Gentile believers are still in bondage to the law. This has further divided Christians into separate groups, sects, and denominations.

If only Christians would hear what God has spoken to them during this age, and claim that which God has given to us and let Israel have that which God has promised to them in the covenants, than all who believe in Jesus Christ as Lord and Savior could fellowship one with another. If Christians would rightly divide the Word, then all scriptures would fall into their rightful place. We could resolve all contentions about law and grace, worshipping on Saturday or Sunday, baptism by immersion or sprinkling, salvation by works or by faith, and thousands of other things that keep believers separated.

The apostle to the Gentiles set forth that body of believers who would be saved by faith in the gospel which he preached concerning Christ as a ransom for all as a distinct and separated entity in the eternal plan and purpose of God. All things relating to this body of believers from the time when this grace of God was first shown to him, to the time this body would be completed, is described by Paul in his epistles to the Gentiles as "the mystery."

The fact that the mystery of God referred to by Paul is the express will of God for the Gentiles of this age is declared in Ephesians 3:1-6: *"For this cause I Paul, the prisoner of Jesus Christ for you Gentiles, If ye have heard of the dispensation of the grace of God which is given me to you-ward: How that by revelation he made known unto me the mystery; (as I wrote afore in few words, Whereby, when ye read, ye may understand my knowledge in the mystery of Christ) Which in other ages was not made known unto the sons of men, as it is now revealed unto his holy apostles and prophets by the Spirit; That the Gentiles should be fellowheirs, and some of the same body, and partakers of his promise in Christ by the gospel."*

The truth that this mystery was made known only to Paul is also presented in Ephesians 3:8-9: *"Unto me, who am less than the least of all saints, is this grace given, that I should preach among the Gentiles the unsearchable riches of Christ; And to make all men see what is the fellowship of the mystery, which from the beginning of the world hath been hid in God, who created all things by Jesus Christ."*

Inasmuch as God the Father created all things by the Son, this mystery body in the sense that it is a new creation destined to inherit heavenly places would naturally concern the person of Jesus Christ. The Old

Testament revealed that the Gentiles, as nations, would be blessed through Israel, which they will. But this forming out of the Gentiles such a body as the church, to be raised in resurrection power and sit with the Lord in the celestial realm was not revealed to the prophets. Such a body would be hid from the understanding of those of former dispensations for it concerned the truth that this raised and glorified assembly would be created in faith out of those who had accepted what Christ had already done for them.

That this mystery had been kept a secret from all men since before the world began, and that it concerned the person of Jesus Christ as revealed in Paul's gospel, to make known to all nations for their obedience in faith, is set forth in Romans 16:25-26: *"Now to him that is of power to stablish you according to my gospel, and the preaching of Jesus Christ, according to the revelation of the mystery, which was kept secret since the world began, But now is made manifest, and by the scriptures of the prophets, according to the commandment of the everlasting God, made known to all nations for the obedience of faith."*

To this living special creation, of which Paul described himself as the first, members are added as they accept by faith that gospel concerning Christ which the Lord gave Paul to preach to the Gentiles. In this body there is neither sexual distinction, racial distinction, national distinction, Jew or Gentile, ignorant men or well-educated men, dumb or smart, black or white, for this body is of Christ. If we had some of our intellect, racial heritage, or even some of our works in it, then it would not all be of Christ but some of ourselves would be in it. *"Lie not one to another, seeing that ye have put off the old man with his deeds; And have put on the new man, which is renewed in knowledge after the image of him that created him: Where there is neither Greek nor Jew, circumcision nor uncircumcision, Barbarian, Scythian, bond nor free: but Christ is all, and in all"* (Col. 3:9-11).

According to the mystery of the church committed to Paul, the hope of our eternal glory is Jesus Christ, and because we are in Christ and Christ is in us, our future cannot be separated from that which belongs to the risen and glorified Son of God. *"Whereof I am made a minister, according to the dispensation of God which is given to me for you, to fulfil the word of God; Even the mystery which hath been hid from ages and from generations, but now is made manifest to his saints: To whom God would make known what is the riches of the glory of this mystery among the Gentiles; which is Christ in you, the hope of glory"* (Col. 1:25-27).

The mystery which was given to Paul concerning the church also entailed the indwelling of the Holy Spirit in each member of the body, securing the believer firmly in Christ until the Head is eternally united to the body. *"In whom we have redemption through his blood, the forgiveness of sins, according to the riches of his grace; Wherein he hath abounded toward us in all wisdom and prudence; Having made known unto us the mystery of his will, according to his good pleasure which he hath purposed in himself: That in the dispensation of the fulness of times he might gather together in one all things in Christ, both which are in heaven, and which are on earth; even in him: In whom also we have obtained an inheritance, being predestinated according to the purpose of him who worketh all things after the counsel of his own will: That we should be to the praise of his glory, who first trusted in Christ. In whom we also trusted, after that ye heard the word of truth, the gospel of your salvation: in whom also after that ye believed, ye were sealed with that holy Spirit of promise, Which is the earnest of our inheritance until the redemption of the purchased possession, unto the praise of his glory"* (Eph. 1:7-14).

Paul entreated Christians to diligently seek out the

depth of this mystery revealed in his epistles whereby they would know the extent of the glory and riches awaiting them in Christ. We are informed in Philippians 3:9-14 that this heritage awaiting the body of Christ through the power of his resurrection is not according to the self-righteousness of the law, but only by that righteousness of God which comes by faith in Christ. So boundless and glorious was this heritage that was revealed to Paul that he counted all his knowledge, education, political, and religious position in the Sanhedrin, all the riches that would have been his, and all the family relations and ties, but as dung in view of that which lay before him in Christ.

This is what God has determined for the church before the foundation of the world. Thus, it could not be according to the law or part of the covenants God made with Israel. Why should we try to lay claim to part of the Kingdom on earth, when we, as partakers of the mystery revealed to Paul, will be in Christ over all things?

The relation of the church to Christ as His body is described in Ephesians 1:20-23: *"...he wrought in Christ, when he raised him from the dead, and set him at his own right hand in the heavenly places, Far above all principality, and power, and might, and dominion, and every name that is named, not only in this world, but also in that which is to come: And hath put all things under his feet, and gave him to be the head over all things to the church, Which is his body, the fulness of him that filleth all in all."*

When we say "church" to what do we refer? In the original Greek, the word *curiake* when used for church meant a building, "House of God." The Greek word *ecclesia* meant the inclusive members of an organization. There are all kinds of churches. The children of Israel in the wilderness, even though they certainly were not part of the mystery revealed to Paul, were called a church in the New Testament. Today, we have the Buddhist church, the Islamic church, and all kinds of churches. These religious organizations are called churches in the media. However, there is only one church in the Bible that is referred to as the body of Christ, and that is the church, or living organism, of all believers who have been saved by faith in Jesus Christ, apart from the covenants. As to whether the Jewish church at Jerusalem operating under the gospel of the Kingdom constituted a part of this body of Christ or not is a debatable question on which many disagree.

The twelve apostles were promised by Christ that they would sit upon twelve thrones during the Kingdom age, ruling over the twelve tribes of Israel. No specific Kingdom promise is made to Christians as we shall be with Christ, over all things, including Israel. As the destruction of the Temple approached, Peter, in his last epistle, did point to the epistles of Paul and Jesus Christ as having taken the sins of the world upon Himself on the cross. John, writing after the destruction of the Temple, presented Christ as the Sin-bearer. He appropriates salvation in Christ in the present tense. As to whether all, part, or none of the members of the Jerusalem church remained as children of the Kingdom, heirs of the promises of the fathers, or whether all, part, or none were included in the body of Christ in which there is neither Jew nor Gentile, is a question, as far as the purposes of this particular study are concerned, that should be left with God.

Today, some churches proclaim a kingdom on earth in which their memberships will become God's administrators. Some teach that the New Testament church has inherited all the Old Testament promises and covenants of Israel. Some teach that the sole purpose of the church is to improve the social order. However, few are teaching that even before the foundation of this present world, the Creator ordained that from the human race He would call from Planet Earth a redeemed and sanctified body of men and women from all nations and races to inherit the heavens and rule and reign with His only begotten Son, Jesus Christ, forever. This is that mystery which was hidden from the understanding of all men until it was revealed to the Apostle Paul, the apostle to the Gentiles. Failure to understand and teach the expressed uniqueness of the church of the dispensation of grace has also divided Christendom into even more divisions.

This one promise of God, that Christians shall sit, or inhabit with Jesus Christ, in heavenly places shall be fulfilled. To borrow a phrase from *Star Trek*: **"We shall boldly go where no man has gone before."**

Chapter Thirteen

The Galatian Apostasy

"Paul, an apostle, (not of men, neither by man, but by Jesus Christ, and God the Father, who raised him from the dead;) And all the brethren which are with me, unto the churches of Galatia: Grace be to you and peace from God the Father, and from our Lord Jesus Christ, Who gave himself for our sins, that he might deliver us from this present evil world, according to the will of God and our Father: To whom be glory for ever and ever. Amen" (Gal. 1:1-5).

In 278 B.C., a warlike Japhetic race of people known as the Gauls, who occupied much of the southern part of Europe, left their homes and traveled eastward. They passed through the region of Europe now known as Yugoslavia, and they settled temporarily in Macedonia and Greece. This did not meet the approval of the Macedonians and the Greeks, and they were forced still farther eastward into what is now central Turkey, from the Mediterranean Sea to the Black Sea. Here they integrated with the natives of the region and formed their own social order, even though much of the culture and religion of the area was merged into their own political and religious beliefs. This area, which lay to the east of the provinces of Togarmah and Asia, became known as Galatia, the land of the Gauls. History indicates they were even welcomed into Galatia by King Nicomedes to help him fight a civil war.

According to Daniel 4:17, the sovereignty of God is

absolute in the affairs of men and nations. Also, it is declared by Paul in Acts 17:26 that God has determined from the beginning, the bounds and habitations of nations on the face of the earth. As to why God allowed this strange migration, or what possessed the Gauls to leave their beautiful homeland and settle in a semi-desert and rugged region in what is now Asia Minor, we can only conclude that it was according to His will, to complete His eternal plan and purpose. God's covenant with Noah was that His primary blessing would be upon the descendants of Shem. A secondary blessing was given to the descendants of Japheth, in that they would be enlarged. During the dispensation of God's sovereign grace, Japheth has been the primary recipient of the Gospel of Jesus Christ, and Japheth has been enlarged. The Galatians were a transitional link in the passing of the Gospel from Asia to Europe. It was in Galatia that Paul preached the Gospel to peoples of Japhetic origin, and from Galatia he went westward into Macedonia with the revelation that God gave him for the Gentiles.

Paul made three missionary journeys into Galatia (Acts 13:1-14; Acts 15:36-38; Acts 16:1-6). He went through southern Galatia on all three journeys, and on one journey he went into northern Galatia. Little is known about any congregations he established in northern Galatia; however, the scriptural account lists several churches that were founded in the south, and it was doubtless to these churches at Lystra, Iconium, Derbe, Antioch, and even Colosse and possibly Laodicea, that the epistle to the churches at Galatia was intended.

The purpose of the epistle of Paul to the Galatians concerns the purity of the Pauline revelation from God to the Gentiles; to wit, that Jesus Christ appeared personally to Paul for the specific purpose of giving

Paul a message to be proclaimed to the Gentile world. This message came by the grace of God to be accepted, not on the basis of former covenants with mankind through Israel, but by faith and faith alone. And so it was the calling of Paul and the revelation of Jesus Christ to Paul that came under attack in Galatia by men who came down from Jerusalem. The epistle to the Galatians still needs to be studied and proclaimed today, not only because all Scripture is given by inspiration of God and is profitable in all things, but particularly so because many churches continue to be ensnared in the Galatian error: mixing Judaism and Christianity--law and grace.

The epistle to the Galatians was written in A.D. 58, the same year Paul wrote to the Christians at Rome. Both epistles were written in the last year of Paul's freedom to engage in missionary campaigns. The following year he was arrested in Jerusalem at the Temple, and subsequently sent to Rome at the apostle's own request.

The basic foundational Gospel entities covered by Paul in his salutation to the church members in Galatia were:

1. **Paul's defense of his apostleship**--An apostle is one who is sent by another to act in the sender's behalf. Some, and especially members of the Pharisees who had come to profess Christ, denied that Paul was an apostle because Paul did not believe in Jesus until three years after the crucifixion. They claimed that Paul had no authority to preach a new message or to interpret doctrine apart from that authority given him by the Jerusalem assembly. Paul's defense of his apostleship, and his right to declare the gospel of grace to the Gentiles, lay in his claim that Jesus Christ appeared to him in a bright light, witnessed by the

company of soldiers that he led. It was at that time that Christ appointed Paul to be His apostle to the Gentiles. The Lord gave him specific instructions concerning what he should preach to the Gentiles for their salvation and sanctification. In Paul's first two epistles (1 Thessalonians and 2 Thessalonians) he made only one brief reference to his apostleship. But it was after the writing of the first two epistles that his ministry came under attack, and in every epistle written afterward, he stoutly defended his calling, no less than twenty-five times. The message of grace through faith that Paul preached to the Gentiles rested upon his being called in person by Jesus Christ. If Paul did not actually see Jesus on the road to Damascus, then he had no authority to preach to the Gentiles except by permission of the Jerusalem church.

2. **The resurrection of Jesus Christ**--The resurrection of Jesus Christ is set forth clearly in the four gospels by Matthew, Mark, Luke, and John. It was not only declared by Peter in Acts, but also in his epistles (1 Pet. 1:3). James and Jude both alluded to the return of Jesus Christ, which would of course mean that He first arose from the grave. And even though the resurrection of Jesus Christ is boldly declared by others, no other writer of New Testament Scripture is more thorough and systematic in establishing the certainty of Christ's resurrection than Paul. If Jesus Christ did not rise literally and bodily from the grave, then the Person in the bright light that Paul saw was not the Lord and there was no special gospel from God to preach to the Gentiles, and as he wrote in the fifteenth chapter of 1 Corinthians, "...then is our preaching vain...we are of all men most miserable."

3. **A prayer for the grace of God and peace through**

Jesus Christ to be with the Galatian churches--Grace is an unearned, undeserved favor from God. Paul reminded all the churches in every epistle that salvation is by faith through God's grace. Paul wrote in Romans 5:1, *"...being justified by faith, we have peace with God through our Lord Jesus Christ."* Paul wrote further that all the unsaved are at war with God, enemies of God, and the only way peace with God can be made is to accept His terms for peace--unconditional surrender to faith in Jesus Christ who died for their sins (transgressions against God) on the cross.

These three basic truths concerning Jesus Christ and the gospel that Paul had been given for their salvation was restated by the apostle for the purpose of introducing his next statement. *"I marvel that ye are so soon removed from him that called you into the grace of Christ unto another gospel: Which is not another; but there be some that trouble you, and would pervert the gospel of Christ. But though we, or an angel from heaven, preach any other gospel unto you than that which we have preached unto you, let him be accursed. As we said before, so say I now again, If any man preach any other gospel unto you than that ye have received, let him be accursed"* (Gal. 1:6-9).

It had only been a few months since Paul had visited the churches in Galatia, probably no more than three years at most. And we read of the churches in Galatia in Acts 16:5, *"And so were the churches established in the faith, and increased in number daily."* Now then, what happened? Paul provides a brief outline of the reasons for their decline in the first chapter, verses six through nine:

1. **Removed themselves from the doctrinal position set forth by Paul concerning the cross**--Paul wrote the

church at Corinth that he purposed to know nothing among them save Jesus Christ and Him crucified. This was the message he also preached in Galatia-- Christ died for our sins according to the Scriptures. But Paul now wrote to them that he marvelled that they were so soon removed from the doctrine of salvation by faith through grace in the death of Christ for sin. The word "removed" comes from the Greek *metatithemi* which means a turncoat, or in religious terminology, an apostate. So the trouble at Galatia was not just carnality or spiritual poverty, but rank apostasy because they had been led to reject the gospel preached to them by Paul, and accept the false proposition that the atonement offered by Christ on the cross was not enough to save them.

2. **Turning to another gospel**--When you turn from something, you will turn toward something. This is why God admonishes Christians to be steadfast in the faith of Christ and not be blown about by every wind of doctrine. An ill doctrinal wind had blown through Galatia, and like a weather vane, turned them around to another gospel, which Paul said was no gospel. Gospel simply means "good news." God had good news for Noah in that He instructed the pre-flood patriarch to build an ark so that his family would be saved. God had good news for Abraham in that He told the father of the Hebrews to get out of Ur and all the nations of earth would be blessed through his seed. God had good news for Israel in bondage in that if they would follow Moses and obey the command-ments, He would give them a land flowing with milk and honey for an everlasting inheritance. And Abraham, as well as all the other heroes of faith in the Old Testament, believed that what God had prom-ised He would perform, and their faith was counted

unto them for righteousness (Rom. 4:20-22). Paul did not tell the Galatians to build an ark, look for a city, or strike out for the promised land. He did tell them that Jesus Christ had given him some good news to relate to all men, and this good news was, believe on the Lord Jesus Christ and they would be saved from the penalty of sin (eternal death) unto eternal life. But someone else had entered into the churches of Galatia and told the church members that God had given to *them* the good news for this age. According to this so-called new gospel, their faith in Christ was all right, but it was not enough to save them from their sins. They must also be circumcised and obey the letter of the law of Moses, which by this time had been supplemented by hundreds of Jewish ordinances. But Paul related in his epistle to these churches that this other gospel was really no gospel. It was not good news; it was bad news. It was bad news because it was impossible. Paul knew it was impossible because there is no way a man can either add to or take away from the finished work that Christ perfected through His death. *"For by grace are ye saved through faith; and that not of yourselves: it is the gift of God: Not of works, lest any man should boast"* (Eph. 2:8-9).

In verses ten through twelve of the first chapter of Galatians, Paul again affirms that the gospel which he brought to the Galatians was a message directly given to him by Jesus Christ. It did not come from the Jerusalem church, nor did anyone at Jerusalem have any authority to interpret or amend it.

"But of these who seemed to be somewhat, (whatsoever they were, it maketh no matter to me: God accepteth no man's person:) for they who seemed to be somewhat in conference added nothing to me: But contrariwise, when they saw that the

gospel of the uncircumcision was committed unto me, as the gospel of the circumcision was unto Peter; (For he that wrought effectually in Peter to the apostleship of the circumcision, the same was mighty in me toward the Gentiles:) And when James, Cephas, and John, who seemed to be pillars, perceived the grace that was given unto me, they gave to me and Barnabas the right hands of fellowship; that we should go unto the heathen, and they unto the circumcision. Only they would that we should remember the poor; the same which I also was forward to do" (Gal. 2:6-10). The points of interest to us, stressed by Paul in these five verses are:

1. **Nothing added to the Pauline revelation**--From Acts 15:6-7, and according to the words of Paul in verse six of the second chapter of Galatians, the elders of the Jerusalem church, with a show of self-importance, went into conference to decide whether the Gentiles were going to have to be circumcised and keep the law. Paul stated they made a show of importance, but he was not impressed, because God looks on the inward man rather than on the outward appearance. Even though Paul had gone up to Jerusalem to get a ruling from the Jerusalem church, it appears he had no affinity for the conference. God had given him the message to preach to the Gentiles; therefore, he seemed to reason, how could these members of the Jerusalem church add to or take away something from the Lord. Therefore, he refused to concede they had any right to add to or take from the gospel he preached to the Gentiles. The apostle mentioned in verse ten that the Jerusalem church asked him to prevail upon the Gentile Christians to remember the poor, and Paul stated that he always did this one thing anyway, so it was really a useless request. However, in

going back to the Jerusalem conference in the fifteenth chapter of Acts, Luke mentions that the elders and apostles in Jerusalem also asked that for the sake of Jews in Gentile cities, the Gentile believers also abstain from eating meats from strangled animals, from meats sacrificed to idols, from eating animal blood, and from fornication. In his epistles to the church at Corinth, Paul condemned both idol worship and fornication, but the reason he overlooked these particular deliberations of the Jerusalem conference in Galatians would appear that he did not want to give the churches of Galatia any reason to conclude that the Jewish church at Jerusalem, or any member of that church including Peter, James, and John, had any authority over his apostleship, or that they could add anything to the Gospel of Jesus Christ according to God's grace, which he preached among the Gentile world for obedience in faith.

2. **The two gospels--the gospels of Circumcision and Uncircumcision**--Paul said that any who would construe that he had compromised with the Jerusalem assembly concerning his ministry to the Gentiles would be wrong. In fact, just the opposite is true. There was a recognition between all concerned that God had given Peter a message to preach to the Jews, and God had given him (Paul) a message to preach to the Uncircumcision. Was there an actual difference between the gospel of Circumcision committed to Peter and the gospel of Uncircumcision committed to Paul? Certainly there is much disagreement on this subject, but it is our sincere opinion there is a difference, else it would have made no difference if Peter preached to the Gentiles and Paul to the Jews.

"But when Peter was come to Antioch, I withstood him to

*the face, because he was to be blamed. For before that certain
came from James, he did eat with the Gentiles: but when they
were come, he withdrew and separated himself, fearing them
which were of the circumcision. And the other Jews dissembled
likewise with him; insomuch that Barnabas also was carried
away with their dissimulation. But when I saw that they walked
not uprightly according to the truth of the gospel, I said unto
Peter before them all, If thou, being a Jew, livest after the
manner of Gentiles, and not as do the Jews, why compellest thou
the Gentiles to live as do the Jews? We who are Jews by nature,
and not sinners of the Gentiles, Knowing that a man is not
justified by the works of the law, but by the faith of Jesus Christ,
even we have believed in Jesus Christ, that we might be justified
by the faith of Christ, and not by the works of the law: for by the
works of the law shall no flesh be justified. But if, while we seek
to be justified by Christ, we ourselves also are found sinners, is
therefore Christ the minister of sin? God forbid. For if I build
again the things which I destroyed, I make myself a transgres-
sor"* (Gal. 2:11-18). The points of interest that are to be
remembered in these eight verses of scripture are:

1. **The hypocrisy of Peter**--From the context it is easily
   determined that Peter visited the Gentile church at
   Antioch, the home church of Paul and Barnabas. It is
   possible that Peter even accompanied Paul when he
   returned from the Jerusalem council. Of course, we
   remember that by God's special leading, Peter had
   formerly preached to Cornelius and his family, but
   Cornelius was a godly man, a Gentile well liked in
   Israel because he was a friend of the Jews. This
   actually opened the door for a more liberal acceptance of Gentiles by the Jerusalem church; but still,
   Peter took a host of witnesses back to prove that he
   acted only upon the commandment of God, and the
   Holy Spirit had been given to this Gentile household.

And so Peter, full of the spirit of fellowship that seemed to be manifested at the Jerusalem council, went down to Antioch and boldly sat down with the Gentile membership and even ate with them at meals. News of this strange behavior, that was contrary to normal Jewish behavior, was carried back up to the Jerusalem church. James, who by this time was at least a co-equal with Peter in authority, sent some delegates down to Antioch to determine if this were really true. They doubtless timed their visit to coincide with one of the meal times, and sure enough, there was Peter eating elbow to elbow with the Gentile membership. And not only that, but there were some Jewish Christians also eating with Gentile Christians. Whether these Jewish believers were members of the Antioch church is not made clear. In most non-Jewish churches, there were a few Jewish believers. Luke, in recounting the events of Paul's ministry, usually records that some, or a few, Jews were saved, and a great many, or multitude, Greeks or Gentiles were saved. So most, if not all, the Gentile churches contained a few Jewish believers. However, Peter moved away from the Gentiles when men sent by James appeared. The Greek text indicates that Peter made a big hypocritic show, or feigned indignation, to such an extent that the Jewish believers likewise moved away from their Gentile brethren. The word for dissimulation literally means the actions of hypocrites. Now how do you think these Gentile Christians felt? Paul suddenly had a divided church. He had to act quickly and forcefully, and there are times in a church, or a Christian organization, when such action is not only justified, but necessary. Verses eleven and fourteen of the second chapter of Galatians relate that Paul got up and withstood Peter to his face before the entire congregation, because it is evident in verse fourteen that Peter began telling the Gentiles they had to keep the law of Moses and refrain from eating certain meats. Paul's rebuttal of Peter's blasphemy and hypocrisy was made more difficult, because even Barnabas who had been Paul's companion on missionary journeys to preach the Gospel to the Gentiles, went over and stood with Peter. Augustine said, *"It is not advantageous to correct in secret an error which injured openly."* So Paul did not ask Peter and Barnabas to meet him secretly in conference to settle the matter. The error had been made in public assembly, so Paul dealt with it in the open assembly. *"Knowing that a man is not justified by the works of the law, but by the faith of Jesus Christ, even we have believed in Jesus Christ, that we might be justified by the faith of Christ, and not by the works of the law: for by the works of the law shall no flesh be justified. But if, while we seek to be justified by Christ, we ourselves also are found sinners, is therefore Christ the minister of sin? God forbid"* (Gal. 2:16-17). In these two verses Paul continued his condemnation of the stand taken by Paul and Barnabas at Antioch in order to expose the error of those who deceived the churches in Galatia.

2. **Law and grace do not mix**--Peter, Barnabas, and the Jewish believers at Antioch, all, according to Paul, had placed their faith in Jesus Christ for justification before God. But if Jesus Christ is not able to keep the Christian righteous before God, and if Christians can fall into a lost condition, or they have to obey rules and ordinances to keep themselves saved, then according to the apostle, Jesus Christ becomes a minister of sin. A man cannot work, either by law or conscience, to save himself from sin. And a point that Paul makes is that neither can a man work to keep his salvation. If a Christian has to work to keep his

salvation, then Paul said that Jesus Christ lied. Works are the result of salvation--not a part of it. Works are the evidence of salvation.

"O foolish Galatians, who hath bewitched you, that ye should not obey the truth, before whose eyes Jesus Christ hath been evidently set forth, crucified among you? This only would I learn of you, Received ye the Spirit by the works of the law, or by the hearing of faith? Are ye so foolish? having begun in the Spirit, are ye now made perfect by the flesh? Have ye suffered so many things in vain? if it be yet in vain. He therefore that ministereth to you the Spirit, and worketh miracles among you, doeth he it by the works of the law, or by the hearing of faith?" (Gal. 3:1-5). In the first five verses of the third chapter of Galatians, two points of interest are emphasized:

1. **The hypnotic effect of false teachers**--Paul begins the third chapter with a note of surprised indignation-- "O foolish Galatians, who hath bewitched you." The Greek word for bewitched at the time Paul wrote the epistle meant controlling someone for evil purposes. The agent from which the evil sprang was the Devil, or demons, and the expression used to designate such influence was the "evil eye." It is very close to what we would refer to today as being hypnotized. So what Paul actually meant was: Who has hypnotized you and put you under an evil spell? This illustrates the evil, hypnotic effect that false teachers can have upon Christians. We read in 2 Corinthians 11:13-14, *"For such are false apostles, deceitful workers, transforming themselves into the apostles of Christ. And no marvel; for Satan himself is transformed into an angel of light."* The charge of Paul is that the Galatian church members had been mesmerized and put under an evil spell. He could only conclude this to be true, because they had

turned from Jesus Christ and Him crucified for righteousness, back to the law. Paul said there was no excuse, therefore it had to be an evil spell, because he had set forth Jesus Christ and Him crucified among them. The word for "set forth" in the Greek is *prographo*, which means placard, or photograph in modern terminology. Today, Paul would say that he had posted the message of salvation through faith in Jesus Christ on every billboard in town. Paul's account of the error that befell the churches in Galatia demonstrates how Satan works through his agents in the churches to corrupt entire congregations.

2. **Evidence of the Holy Spirit is proof of eternal justification**--In verses two and three of the third chapter of Galatians, Paul, giving evidence of his legal background, presents an indisputable argument. He refers back to the beginning of their Christian testimony when they accepted Christ as Savior, when they began "in the Spirit." The Holy Spirit came into their lives because of their faith in Christ. Paul indicates that the Holy Spirit came when they believed that Christ was crucified for their sins. The Holy Spirit did not come because of some work they did, or because they obeyed the commandments. The Spirit came because of their faith in Christ, but now they were going to try to improve on the work of the Holy Spirit with their own works. Paul wrote to them that they were foolish, because the Holy Spirit had done a perfect job on which they could not improve--created them all-new creatures in Christ, forever. This Gospel truth is declared over and over in the New Testament. For example, in Ephesians 1:13-14 we read, *"In whom ye also trusted, after that ye heard the word of truth, the gospel of your salvation: in whom also after that ye believed, ye were sealed with that holy Spirit of*

promise, Which is the earnest of our inheritance until the redemption of the purchased possession, unto the praise of his glory." So God seals our salvation through the Holy Spirit so that all the glory is His and none is ours. If we had to work to keep our salvation sealed, then part of the glory would be ours, and that is contrary to Scripture.

"*For as many of you as have been baptized into Christ have put on Christ. There is neither Jew nor Greek, there is neither bond nor free, there is neither male nor female: for ye are all one in Christ Jesus. And if ye be Christ's, then are ye Abraham's seed, and heirs according to the promise*" (Gal. 3:27-29). The three concluding doctrinal issues stressed by Paul in chapter three are:

1. **All Christians are baptized into Christ**--Being baptized into the body of Jesus Christ in no way implies water baptism. A person can be baptized with water a million times, and he will still not be baptized into Christ. Nowhere in his letter to the Galatians did Paul even refer to water baptism, but he did in several places speak of the coming of the Holy Spirit into the lives of believers at the time they received Jesus Christ by faith. Paul here speaks of all races, social classes, and sexes being baptized into Christ, and the meaning is made clearer in 1 Corinthians 12:13, "*For by one Spirit are we all baptized into one body, whether we be Jews or Gentiles, whether we be bond or free....*" To try to make the baptism of Galatians 3:27 water baptism, is to knowingly pervert the Word of God. Paul also said that to be baptized into Jesus Christ by the Holy Spirit is to put on Christ. One of the common usages of the word "baptism" in Greece applied to women dipping their clothes in a vat of dye. They would immerse the

cloth in the dye, and naturally it would put on the color of the dye after it was brought up out of the water. This symbolizes the baptism of the Holy Spirit. The Holy Spirit baptizes the believer into Jesus Christ so that the new Christian may put on the nature of Christ.

2. **In the Body of Christ all are made as one**--Peter led the revolt in the church at Antioch that separated Jew from Gentile, and so to forever set the record straight, Paul states without qualification that in Christ there is neither race, color, class, nor sex.

3. **Abraham's seed by adoption**--Christians are Abraham's seed, because Jesus Christ is Abraham's seed according to the promise, and God has adopted us through His Son. Abraham's promise was heavenly in that he looked for a heavenly city promised by God, and by faith we Christians also look for a heavenly promise--to sit with Jesus Christ in heavenly places (Eph. 3:10; 2:6).

"And because ye are sons, God hath sent forth the Spirit of his Son into your hearts, crying, Abba, Father. Wherefore thou art no more a servant, but a son; and if a son, then an heir of God through Christ. Howbeit then, when ye knew not God, ye did service unto them which by nature are no gods. But now, after that ye have known God, or rather are known of God, how turn ye again to the weak and beggarly elements, whereunto ye desire again to be in bondage? Ye observe days, and months, and times, and years. I am afraid of you, lest I have bestowed upon you labour in vain" (Gal. 4:6-11). The doctrinal points of interest in these verses are:

1. **Christians are children of God**--In verse six Paul declares that the Holy Spirit testifies to the Christian that he is a son of God--not *"the"* son of God, because

there is only one "begotten" Son--Jesus Christ. The word for "crying" in the Greek text used of the Holy Spirit coming into the Christian's heart does not mean crying in the sense of weeping. Instead, it means to proclaim important or joyous news, like a town crier making a public pronouncement. So the Holy Spirit brings the good news into the believer's heart that by faith in Jesus Christ he has become a child of God, not a baby or minor in the sense of being under a guardian, but an adult heir whereby Christians may go directly to the Father. And so Paul asks the Galatians why they would exchange the privilege of going directly into the presence of God, to their former status of begging crumbs from the master's table at the door of the servants.

2. **Apostasy**--Paul brings out to the Galatians that one error leads to another error. If they had gone back under the law of Moses, how long would it be before they returned to heathenish practices of idol worship? In fact, Paul gives evidence that this was already happening. Paul stressed that he had become afraid of the Galatian Christians. Martin Luther said of this verse, *"These words of Paul breathe tears."* Paul was not afraid that they would lose their salvation, but he feared that in their going back to observing the feasts of Israel, and pagan holidays, God would no longer honor their testimony and the apostle's investment of his time and service in them would become in vain. Some Christians today have the idea that in these early churches, members were all filled with the Holy Ghost, love, and brotherhood, and they went everywhere speaking in tongues and healing the sick. This is not exactly the way it was. Most of them had problems--doctrinal problems, authority problems, and moral problems. The Devil is never silent when

it God is at work.

"Stand fast therefore in the liberty wherewith Christ hath made us free, and be not entangled again with the yoke of bondage. Behold, I Paul say unto you, that if ye be circumcised, Christ shall profit you nothing. For I testify again to every man that is circumcised, that he is a debtor to do the whole law. Christ is become of no effect unto you, whosoever of you are justified by the law; ye are fallen from grace. For we through the Spirit wait for the hope of righteousness by faith. For in Jesus Christ neither circumcision availeth any thing, nor uncircumcision; but faith which worketh by love" (Gal. 5:1-6). The truths to be stressed in these first six verses of the fifth chapter are:

1. **Christians are to stand fast in the liberty of Christ-**Paul brings out in the first verse that the Galatians were in jeopardy of losing their liberty in Christ, because they were in danger of becoming entangled in the yoke of bondage--the law. The word for entangled in the Greek means to be ensnared, or lured into a trap. The trap in this particular case was circumcision. The members of the Galatian churches had professed Jesus Christ as Lord and Savior on the premise that He had died for their sins. However, the false teachers from the church at Jerusalem told them that Christ died only for the sins that are past, but to keep themselves justified concerning future sins they must keep the law. In other words, unless they wore the yoke of bondage of the law, they would be lost just as if they had never believed in Jesus Christ. And so Paul pleads with the memberships of those churches to stay free of this yoke, this spiritual trap.

2. **To keep the letter of the law is to fall from grace--**In verse four, Paul explained to the Galatians that Christ

becomes of no effect to those who attempt to keep the law, or depend upon their own works for justification. This means that Jesus Christ had no effect on their daily Christian lives. They did not show forth the Lord Jesus in their relationship to others. As verse three teaches also, once a person commits himself to keep the law (which also includes depending upon works for salvation), then such a person is bound to keep every commandment of the law. This truth is also declared in James 2:10, *"For whosoever shall keep the whole law, and yet offend in one point, he is guilty of all."* The law includes such things as jealousy, envy, gossip (spreading lies or bearing false witness against a neighbor). Jesus said that if a man even looked on a woman and desired her in his heart, that man had broken the law against adultery. Of course, if a Christian is trying to keep himself saved, there would go his salvation. If he died before he repented, according to the false teachers that plagued the Galatians, he would go to Hell. Such a theology indicates that a Christian can be saved one day and lost the next, and the believer should pray that he dies on the day he is saved. All are born in sin, falling through space toward eternal perdition. Let us suppose a man calls out to Jesus Christ to save him, and the Lord reaches out to him, but instead of returning the man to solid ground, Jesus would place him where the man could grab hold of the edge of the precipice. Then the Lord would say to the man, "I have saved you from falling, but now it is up to you to hang on, or you will fall again." This would not be salvation, but a mockery. *"...I give unto them eternal life; and they shall never perish, neither shall any man pluck them out of my hand"* (John 10:28). *"...this is the record, that God hath given to us eternal life, and this life is in his Son"*

(1 John 5:11). This promise is in the present tense, an eternal life means unforfeitable. If we can lose it, or someone can take it away, then it is not eternal. But Paul said that those who depend upon works, or the works of the law, to keep their salvation, had fallen from grace. However, note the wording, *"...ye are fallen from grace."* This means that the Galatians had lost faith in the strength of God's grace to keep them saved. A Christian is not only saved by grace, but he is kept by grace. This truth is declared in Romans 5:1-2, *"Therefore being justified by faith, we have peace with God through our Lord Jesus Christ: By whom also we have access by faith into this grace wherein we stand...."* It is up to the Christian to avail himself of the depths of God's grace on a daily basis. Paul, in recounting his many trials, tribulations, and afflictions in Christian service, looked to God and said, "Thy grace is sufficient." But instead of depending upon God's grace to sustain them in their daily Christian walk, the Galatians had gone back to the strength of the law, which was not strength but weakness. Being fallen from grace, as referred to in Galatians 5:4, in no way relates to the loss of salvation in Christ, but rather to Christian testimony and service.

3. **Circumcision makes no difference**--As far as the act of circumcision is concerned, there is really no spiritual significance to it as far as God is concerned, once Jesus Christ had died for sin on the cross. Today it makes no difference to God whether a man is circumcised or uncircumcised. Circumcision was a sign of the weakness of the flesh, and the law was given to expose and make known to man that by the deeds of the law could no flesh be saved. As brought out by Paul, the error is in binding one's self through circumcision to keep the law for righteousness. Righ-

teousness means a living process in which the individual always does the right thing before God. But Paul brings out in verse five of Galatians 5 that our hope of righteousness in this world is not by keeping the law, but in the same hope by which we were saved--faith in Jesus Christ according to God's grace. Christians through love can keep the law in a spiritual sense more completely than those who were bound to the law before the cross.

"Ye did run well; who did hinder you that ye should not obey the truth? This persuasion cometh not of him that calleth you. A little leaven leaveneth the whole lump. I have confidence in you through the Lord, that ye will be none otherwise minded: but he that troubleth you shall bear his judgment, whosoever he be. And I, brethren, if I yet preach circumcision, why do I yet suffer persecution? then is the offence of the cross ceased. I would they were even cut off which trouble you. For, brethren, ye have been called unto liberty; only use not liberty for an occasion to the flesh, but by love serve one another. For all the law is fulfilled in one word, even in this; Thou shalt love thy neighbour as thyself. But if ye bite and devour one another, take heed that ye be not consumed one of another" (Gal. 5:7-15). The points of interest for our edification in these verses are:

1. **Why handicap yourself in running the Christian race?**--Paul here indicates the church members of the Galatian congregation were running a good Christian race. This terminology of athletic contests in other Pauline epistles refers to a full testimony, spreading the Gospel, faithful in service, and being active ambassadors for Christ. But Paul reminds the Galatians that they now are stumbling and falling on the race track, so he asks, "Who put this handicap on

you? who put this yoke around your necks?" He added further in verse eight that this persuasion, or doctrinal handicap, certainly did not come from God, because why would the Lord put a burden on them when they were running the Christian race so well? The thought here suggested by Paul is that adding anything to the simple message of salvation by grace through faith in Jesus Christ, as far as Christian service is concerned, is like adding burdens to the back of a runner in a race.

2. **A little leaven leaveneth the whole lump**--Leaven is simply yeast, and even a little yeast in dough, if left to ferment long enough under the right conditions, will make the entire lump of dough rise. When the Israelites left Egypt at the exodus, they took unleavened bread, because leavened bread would spoil during the long journey. Therefore, leaven was associated with the sins of Egypt, and Egypt was a type of the world. Thus, leaven became representative of sin. During Passover, leaven was abolished from the entire land, and any Israelite in whose house leaven was found could be put to death. This restriction lasted for the entire Passover season--a full seven days. The meal, or flour offering always followed the sacrificial offering. It never preceded it. The meal offering signified works. Cain offered a meal offering only, indicating that he was depending upon his works. The Passover lamb was a type of Jesus Christ, the sinless Lamb of God who would be offered in our place. The unleavened bread used in the Passover was a type of the sinless body of Jesus Christ. When Jesus passed the unleavened bread and broke it at the Passover supper, He said, "This is my body which is broken for you." This is the doctrine of Christ--the Gospel, or goods news that Jesus Christ, who knew no

sin, died for our sins on the cross. And we are created in Him a new creature unto good works. In other words, we are saved to work, we do not work to be saved, neither do we work to keep our salvation. However, the Bible stresses that our works should be good works, not for the purpose of keeping our salvation, but to glorify Christ. Ephesians 2:8-10 says, *"For by grace are ye saved through faith; and that not of yourselves: it is the gift of God: Not of works, lest any man should boast. For we are his workmanship* [completed by Christ for eternity], *created in Christ Jesus unto good works, which God hath before ordained that we should walk in them."* However, some Christians like those at Galatia who had been sidetracked by false teachers, cares of life, and lusts of the flesh, do not produce good works, as we read in 1 Corinthians 3:11,14-15: *"For other foundation can no man lay than that is laid, which is Jesus Christ....If any man's work abide which he hath built thereupon, he shall receive a reward. If any man's work shall be burned, he shall suffer loss: but he himself shall be saved...."* The relationship of good works to salvation is that they should follow as naturally as May flowers follow April showers. But the error, or leaven, that was introduced into the Galatian churches was corrupting the entire Christian message. Even a little leaven in the meal, relying even a little on the works according to law or conscience, leavens the entire message of the Gospel.

3. **The law is fulfilled in love**--Paul omitted one facet of love mentioned by Jesus Christ, the love of the Lord our God. However, it is understood that Paul was writing to those who had made a profession of faith, and it is assumed that they were Christians, even though they had been deceived into espousing a grave doctrinal error. And what is proposed by Paul,

as verified by many scriptures, is that if we love God as Christians are exhorted, then we will not take the Lord's name in vain, we will not worship other gods, nor will we defile the Temple of the Holy Spirit, or bodies, by giving way to lusts of the flesh. If we love our neighbor as we are instructed in the New Testament, then we will not lie about him, steal his property, murder him, assault his person, or commit adultery or fornication with his wife or daughters. And in considering the lives of the Old Testament characters who were to live by the law, like Saul, David, Solomon, and many others, it is our understanding that Christians do fulfill the commandments of the law in spirit more fully than the Old Testament saints did in trying to keep the letter of the law.

One of the important statements in Paul's epistle to the Galatians is that "a little leaven leaveneth the whole lump." The leaven of the Galatian apostasy spread throughout Christendom. Today it would be difficult to name a single division of Christendom, consisting of hundreds of denominations and almost two billion constituents, that does not in some way contain some contamination from the Galatian heresy. And where did this tragedy begin? As stated by the Apostle Paul, it began with the mixing of the message of the Circumcision that was to be preached to Israel with the message that God gave him to preach to the Uncircumcision.

As long as the message to the Gentiles and the message to the Jewish disciples at Jerusalem were kept separate, there was general unity within the Gentile congregation in Asia. But with the Galatian apostasy, divisions began to spring up, with each division either taking from or adding to the Pauline revelation.

Chapter Fourteen

The Strange Things
Churches Preach

If men claiming ecclesiastical authority were to
appear in your church and announce from the pulpit
that in order for the membership to be saved every male
member would have to immediately be circumcised,
what would the response or reaction be? This is what
occurred at the churches of Galatia, and evidently the
members for the most part were deceived into believing
this absurd teaching. But we know from Paul's epistle to
these churches that the circumcision practiced was not
just a mark in the flesh. It bound these Gentile Christians to keep the whole law given to Israel. It took them
from believing in the grace of God through faith in
Jesus Christ for salvation, to not only keeping the
commandments of God for righteousness, but probably
also returning to sacrificial offerings (Acts 21). But even
as strange as teaching that every male Christian must be
circumcised may be, it is probably that the reader's
church teaches doctrines that may be even more removed from basic New Testament foundational truth.

Paul wrote to the church at Ephesus, *"For by grace
are ye saved through faith; and that not of yourselves: it is the
gift of God: Not of works, lest any man should boast. For we are
his workmanship, created in Christ Jesus unto good works,
which God hath before ordained that we should walk* [live
before the world] *in them. Wherefore remember, that ye*

being in time past Gentiles in the flesh, who are called Uncircumcision by that which is called the Circumcision [Israel] in the flesh made by hands; That at that time ye were without Christ, being aliens from the commonwealth of Israel, and strangers from the covenants of promise, having no hope, and without God in the world: But now in Christ Jesus ye who sometimes [once] *were far off are made nigh* [have come to God] *by the blood of Christ"* (Eph. 2:8-14).

By grace through faith in Jesus Christ who shed His blood (was crucified), Gentiles at Ephesus (and all who believed) were created in the workmanship of God. This being true, how can anything created by God be improved upon? The pope cannot improve upon it; nor can we or angels from Heaven improve upon it. This is God's workmanship, not our workmanship.

However, this perfected, or perfect, workmanship is to walk in, or do good works with the life that is left in the world. Good works can be construed to mean attending church, helping the sick or poor, witnessing, distributing God's Word, praying for others, serving on the mission field, being a godly father or mother, preaching, teaching, being temperate and Christ-like, humble, kind, etc. As Paul plainly stated, Christians walk in, or perform good works because they are saved to work, they do not work to be saved, neither to keep themselves saved. In the beatitudes (Matt. 5:3-12), Jesus Christ was actually referring to Himself, so if Christians want to be more like Jesus Christ, observe the beatitudes, then "great" will be "your reward in heaven."

In reminding the Christians at Ephesus that they were saved by faith through grace in Jesus Christ, the Apostle Paul entreated them to *remember*. Remember what? That they were aliens from the covenants of promise, and once without hope and without God. These Gentile Christians knew nothing about the commandments of the law, the Temple, the feast days, the Passover, Pentecost, the many sacrifices and keeping the Sabbath (Saturday) holy. They had not come to God through the Temple, the sacrifices, the command-ments, or any of the covenants of promise. They had come to God only by and through the blood of Christ, and as the apostle stated in Galatians and all his epistles, why would any Gentile Christian want to place himself under a yoke that even the Jews could not bear? Yet, there is one church today that says if we don't keep Saturday as the Sabbath, we are lost in sin and going into perdition. The Bible plainly states that the Sabbath was a sign to Israel; nowhere does the Bible say Sabbath is a sign to the church.

Paul wrote to the Galatian church members, *"...though we, or an angel from heaven, preach any other gospel unto you than that which we have preached unto you, let him be accursed....If any man preach any other gospel unto you than that that ye have received, let him be accursed."*

The Galatian apostasy spread out from Asia into the known Christian world. Already, as Paul wrote in his epistles to the Corinthians, divisions were springing up in Greece over baptisms and tongues. However, the main problem of the doctrinal error of the Galatian churches was that Jesus Christ could help save a sinner, and help keep Him saved, but He was not all-powerful enough to do it all by Himself without help from the adherent. As this doctrine came to be preached and accepted through repetition and church authority, some began to question that if Jesus Christ was not all-powerful, then He must not be God and Creator. The Gnostic heresy in North Africa infested the churches and the Nestorian branch of Christianity which ques-tioned the Holy Ghost conception of Jesus Christ and the virgin birth spread to the East as far as Xion, China.

The main branch of this doctrine was espoused and proclaimed by a bishop named Arius. By the fourth century dozens of divisions and cults had sprung up. In A.D. 325, Emperor Constantine of the Roman Empire convened the first general ecumenical council at Nicaea. Approximately three hundred bishops and many interested parties, both Christian and non-Christian, attended. While many theological and doctrinal differences were discussed and debated, most went their own way believing exactly the same as when they arrived.

In A.D. 381, Theodosia the Great made Roman Catholic doctrine, as interpreted by the state, the law of the empire. All non-Catholic religions were abolished. At the time it could have been construed to be a good thing, because many of the heretical beliefs were suppressed. However, the church at Rome revived the Galatian heresy by contending that when Jesus committed the keys of the Kingdom to Peter, Peter was given ecclesiastical authority over all the earth, and these keys were passed on to the bishop of Rome, the pope, in continual and successive office. Thus, the pope could admit or turn away from the church and salvation as he willed. Subsequently, the heretical doctrines surrounding the person of Mary developed within the Roman church, election of the saints, indulgences, confessions, pentinence, limbo, and dozens of other false teachings were proposed and included as articles of the Christian faith. At the Fourth Lateran Council of 1215, transubstantiation was declared to be a precept of faith. In 1431, the dogma of purgatory was made a matter of church truth. One after another, extra-biblical and traditional beliefs were added, including papal infallibility.

Recently while teaching combined classes, supported by visuals, in a Catholic high school, I referred to a color slide showing what is believed to be the foundation of Peter's house at Capernaum, Israel. As soon as I asked the students if they knew who the Apostle Peter was, I knew I had made a mistake because in one voice they roared back, "The first pope!" I regrouped by replying to the class's response, "This is where Jesus lived with Peter, Peter's wife, and Peter's mother-in-law."

To make Peter the principal ecclesiastical authority over the early Gentile church is just one of the heretical doctrines of the Roman Catholic Church, which followed after the Galatian apostasy. Even the early Pentecostal church at Jerusalem recognized that Peter's authority was limited to the Circumcision, the Jewish church. Other heretical teachings and doctrines of the Roman Catholic Church are:

Limbo--the abode of the dead for babies or others who may have died without being baptized

Purgatory--a place of temporary punishment after death where believers who have died with unconfessed sins must wait until they receive forgiveness

Indulgences--a writ or permit granted by a church authority to be relieved from punishment for certain sins, often purchased by church members

Prayers to the saints--totally unscriptural

Prayers to Mary--totally unscriptural and heretical

Elevations of the most faithful to sainthood--all Christians by biblical definition are saints

Immaculate conception of Mary--Mary was born in sin the same as everyone except Jesus Christ

Assumption of Mary--a Catholic fabrication

Mary remained a perpetual virgin--According to Matthew 13:55-56, Jesus had four half-brothers and at least two half-sisters, all born to Mary by natural conception and birth

Worship of statues of Mary, Peter, and others--idol worship is forbidden by Scripture

Special revelations and visions from Mary--not so according to Hebrews 1:1-2

Infallibility of the pope--*"If we say that we have no sin, we deceive ourselves, and the truth is not is us"* (1 John 1:8)

Transubstantiation--*"...Who shall ascend into heaven?* [that is, to bring Christ down from above]" (Rom. 10:6)

Masses for the dead--*"...it is appointed unto men once to die, but after this the judgment"* (Heb. 9:27)

Office of priests--Jesus Christ in this age is the only mediator between God and men (1 Tim. 2:5)

Forbidding servants of the church (men and women) to marry--read 1 Timothy 4:3

Forbidding the eating of meat on certain days--read 1 Timothy 4:3 again

The preceding list of Catholic beliefs and teachings is only a part of what we could have enumerated. But why all these basic Catholic articles of faith that have no scriptural base or foundation at all? The reason is quite simple, as explained by Milton v. Blackman, Jr. on pages 35-36 of *Christian Churches of America:*

> *"Roman Catholics teach that in addition to the Bible, tradition is a proper source of religious truth. Unlike Protestants, they also say that the church is the only proper teacher and interpreter of the Bible and that through the church, God has indicated which of the various ancient writings are inspired. Moreover, Roman Catholics teach that tradition is disclosed through the writings of the church fathers, the decisions of general councils, and the decrees of popes."*

In other words, the church has a right to question

and interpret that message which God gave Paul to preach to the Gentiles, but it does not have a right to question or interpret what the pope says. Therefore, doctrines and teachings that have no biblical relationship do not bother most Catholics at all. It was from this kind of heresy that Martin Luther rebelled and most of the non-Catholic churches today are a result of his rebellion against papal authority.

Having said all this, the Roman Catholic Church must be given credit for contending for such important biblical truths as the virgin birth, the Holy Ghost conception of Jesus Christ, the inherent carnality of man, and the sovereignty of God. And, although the Catholic Church considers the Bible only a part of religious truth, it did protect the Scriptures, even though they were chained to the pulpits.

Greek and Russian Orthodox Churches

The Roman Catholic Church and the Greek Orthodox Church both had their doctrinal roots in the state church that Constantine established. However, with the decline and eventual fall of the Roman Empire, the Byzantine Empire with its own state church gradually went its own way and differences evolved in both doctrine and liturgy. When the Byzantine Empire fell to the Ottoman Empire with its own religion in Mohammedanism in 1453, Russia laid claim to the remains of the eastern leg of Rome and the power and prestige of the Byzantine church was transferred to the Russian Orthodox Church.

Because both the Roman Church and the Eastern Orthodox Church rose up out of the same religious system, many of the doctrines, creeds, liturgy, and teachings coincide. The main differences are as follows:

1. All bishops are equal in authority with no one bishop exercising ecclesiastical authority over the others; however, some bishops do have more prestige and power due to reputation and location of their ministry.
2. Statues or idols are rejected for use in worship; however, icons are extensively used and cover the walls of most Eastern Orthodox churches, including the Russian Orthodox churches.
3. Infants and converts are baptized to receive, according to the church, the gifts of the Holy Spirit.
4. Celibacy is required of only the bishops.
5. In the communion service, the bread and wine is mixed together and administered to recipients with a spoon.
6. Most Eastern Orthodox churches reject the immaculate conception of Mary, her assumption, purgatory, limbo, indulgences, and a few other Roman Catholic practices grounded in the edicts of councils and popes.
7. The Greek Orthodox Church and the Russian Orthodox Church agree with the Roman Catholic position on Peter; that Jesus Christ conveyed all authority on earth to the apostle and this authority has been in turn conveyed to the bishops in successive perpetuity.

Accepting the authority committed to Peter under the gospel of the Kingdom rather than the gospel of sovereign grace that was to be preached to the Gentiles, like the Roman Catholic Church, has led to other doctrinal errors held by both Eastern Orthodox bodies.

Protestant and Non-Catholic Churches

There are over two hundred Protestant and non-

Catholic denominations, assemblies, or separate congregations in the United States alone. To attempt to identify the doctrines, teachings, liturgy, and organizational structure of all these churches would take more time and effort than this writer has to offer. Protestant churches differ from non-Catholic churches in that the latter contends they did not emerge from the Protestant Reformation movement of Martin Luther. In fact, many of the non-Catholic churches reject the basic premise of the Protestant Reformation, salvation, and justification by faith. However, many of the non-Catholic denominations like the Southern Baptists, American Baptists, and Northern Baptists, include many of the articles of faith that came out of the Protestant Reformation. Nevertheless, it is acknowledged that without the Protestant Reformation, many of the non-Catholic churches would not be in existence today.

The reasons that non-Catholic churches refuse to be identified with the Protestant Reformation are many, and as noted, some of these reasons are doctrinal. Others contend that their existence pre-dated the Protestant Reformation, like the Anabaptists. Another example is the Church of Christ, which contends that its origin was at the cross when Jesus Christ was crucified.

In A.D. 1510 Martin Luther, a young German monk, made a pilgrimage to Rome. The hypocrisy, licentiousness, and opulence he saw at the Vatican shattered his religious idealism. He returned home with vows to do everything he could to reform his church. In his letters to the pope, bishops, and local Catholic officials, he scathingly denounced every evil practice, including calling Pope Leo the Antichrist.

1. Luther questioned the Catholic priesthood, contending that all Christians were priests of God to minister

to all men.

2. Luther proposed that ordinations to the ministry be under the control and supervision of the local church.

3. Luther questioned the doctrine of apostolic succession, casting doubt upon the office of the pope.

4. Luther rejected the doctrine of substantiation in communion.

5. Luther vehemently denounced the practice of issuing indulgences.

6. Luther denounced the forbidding of ministers of the church to marry. He himself married and his wife bore him children.

7. Luther rejected the idea that salvation depended upon church membership, works, baptism, or obedience to ordinances. He wrote: *"The Christian who is consecrated by his faith does good works, but the works do not make him holier or more Christian, for that is the work of faith alone. And if a man were not first a believer and a Christian, all his works would amount to nothing and would be truly wicked and damnable sins"* (Dillenberger, *Martin Luther*, p. 26).

Martin Luther was eventually excommunicated and would have been burned at the stake for heresy had he not gained local political help and protection. And, it was upon his effort to reform the Catholic Church and bring it back more under the authority of Scripture that the great Protestant Reformation began.

However, with the gradual gaining of political freedom and conscience came an explosion in denominational diversity. Some of these denominations were started by sincere men with a mission to preach the Gospel for the salvation of souls. Others were simply opportunists attempting to gain followings for personal advantage. Obviously, many churches were founded on biblical misinterpretations by the founders taking a few scriptures out of context to try to prove they were the keepers and protectors of God's truth. Even many of our nation's founding fathers, like Benjamin Franklin, were deists, or Unitarians.

Accompanying the explosion of denominational diversity came some religious movements that were outright heretical and occultic:

Mormonism--just a few of the heretical beliefs of Mormons are:
1. There is a Father God and a Mother God.
2. There are many gods in heaven.
3. The Book of Mormon is above the Bible.
4. Polygamy is encouraged.
5. Women go to heaven to bear children for eternity.
6. Apostolic succession--and many other strange beliefs.

Seventh-Day Adventism--some of the past and present beliefs and teachings:
1. Jesus Christ was to return in 1843.
2. The 144,000 sealed Israelites in Revelation will be Seventh-Day Adventists.
3. Teachings and doctrines of the church are based on the one hundred-plus visions of Ellen G. White over a twenty-three year period.
4. Christians should keep the Sabbath (Saturday) holy.
5. In the last days, anyone not keeping the Sabbath will take the mark of the Beast and be lost.
6. The Seventh-Day Adventist church claims that it believes and teaches that salvation is by grace through faith in Jesus Christ and that works follow salvation. By redefining church doctrinal beliefs

like this one, the church hopes to escape occultic identification. However, so much of the church's historical background is rooted in legalism, it is having a difficult time gaining fundamental respectability without denying basic foundational doctrines.

Jehovah Witnesses--some of the doctrines are:
1. Printed its own bible, New World Translation, which reflects Jehovah Witness teachings.
2. Rejects the doctrine of the Trinity.
3. Jesus Christ is the first created son, not co-existent with the Father.
4. Satan, being also a created son, is the brother of Jesus Christ.
5. The Holy Spirit is the will of God, not a Person of the Godhead.
6. Rejects the doctrine of an eternal Hell.
7. Salvation for Jehovah Witnesses is explained in the book *Let God Be True*, p. 298: *"All who by reason of faith in Jehovah God and in Christ Jesus dedicated themselves to do God's will and then faithfully carry out their dedication will be rewarded with everlasting life....However, that life will not be the same for all. The Bible plainly shows that some of these, that is, 144,000, will share in heavenly glory with Christ Jesus, while the others will enjoy the blessings of life down here on earth...."*
8. The most dedicated Jehovah Witnesses (the top 144,000) will inherit heavenly places, the remainder will live in God's kingdom here on earth--thus, their church buildings are called Kingdom Halls.
9. Only Jehovah Witnesses will be saved to inherit eternal life.

Christian Science--some of the history, beliefs, and

teachings:

1. The founder, Mary Baker Eddy, was born in 1821 and suffered from a physical and nervous disability, yet went through three marriages. In later life, she claimed to have found healing through spiritual science and then established the Church of Christ (Scientists). A few of her teachings are:
2. Matter is an illusion of the mind.
3. Satan is a false idea; sin and evil do not exist.
4. Any evidence of death is false--life is real, death is an illusion.
5. God is good; but what is not good does not exist.
6. The Trinity: God the Father-Mother; Christ the spiritual idea of sonship; divine science the Holy Comforter (Eddy, *Trinitarian*, pp. 331-32).
7. Man is the image of God, not matter.
8. Jesus was a man who proposed Christ as an idea.
9. The virgin birth--Jesus Christ was the offspring of Mary's self-conscious communion with God. Any woman can have a child without relations with a man.
10. Science is an image, matter an illusion, there is no sickness or pain.
11. Contemporary constituency of Christian Science is reported to be only about ten thousand. Many reading rooms have been closed.

New Age Movement--the New Age movement, or religion, is actually a revival of the Babel concept. It seems to have its genesis in the Illuminati Society. There is no basic statement of faith, and it appears that anyone can be a New Ager as long as they believe in something other than fundamental Christianity or Orthodox Judaism.

1. In its twentieth century setting, the New Age

religion was promoted through Lucifer Trust by founder Foster Bailey, of New York City, which later changed its name to Lucis Trust in 1922. Lucifer, Lucis, and Illuminati mean light-bearer, light-bringing, or to bear light.

2. The New Age movement declares an approaching millennium called the Aquarian age as the sun passes from the Pisces constellation into the Aquarius constellation. This is occurring at the present time.

3. The New Age, as defined by Lucis Trust, declares many illumined masters like Buddha, Mohammed, Jesus, and others. But the greatest master, identified as Lord Maitreya, will come and bring in the New Age. Lord Maitreya, according to one prominent New Ager, Benjamin Creme, was supposed to have appeared in 1983 but he did not arrive.

4. Lucis Trust and other New Age affiliates have taken out full-page ads in *Reader's Digest* and major magazines and newspapers to champion and advertise the New Age religion, which sometimes reports that the "Christ" is coming.

5. Foster Bailey's work was carried out through his two wives, Mary and Alice. Mary Bailey said in a speech in Seattle, Washington in 1977, "...*the hierarchy of 'superhuman consciousness' are known by various names including The Masters of Wisdom, The Lords of Compassion, and The Society of Illumined Minds who are 'more evolved than we are.'...There are enough of us now to tip the scales.*"

6. New Age religionists generally see god in nature (Mother Earth), holistic health, meditational devotions, environmental causes, UFOs, self, etc. The spiritual base of the New Age is very broad. A New Ager can believe that he or she is god.

7. The New Age religion in its varied tenets is taught

in part in schools, corporation training seminars, churches like St. John Episcopal in New York City, government employee training sessions, the military, etc.

Besides the preceding cults mentioned, there are many more as prominent, or more so, like Scientology, Moonies, Children of God, Yahweh groups, and others. To the list of cults, another long list of occult groups exists like the Church of Satan, Satan worship, witches and warlocks, Masons, etc. To enumerate and doctrinally identify these added cults and occult groups would require an entire book on this one subject.

After the turn of the twentieth century with the explosion of cults, new church divisions, and the introduction of a multitude of new doctrines, doctrinal statements were formed in order to help separate the wheat from the tares. The following doctrinal statement was formulated in 1923 by the Christian Fundamentals Association:

1. We believe in the scriptures of the Old and New Testaments as verbally inspired of God, and inerrant in the original writings, and that they are of supreme and final authority in faith and life.
2. We believe in one God, eternally existing in three persons, Father, Son, and Holy Spirit.
3. We believe that Jesus Christ was begotten by the Holy Spirit, and born of the virgin Mary, and is true God and true man.
4. We believe that man was created in the image of God, that he sinned and thereby incurred not only physical death but also the spiritual death which is separation from God, and that all human beings are born with a sinful nature, and in the case of those who reach

moral responsibility, become sinners in thought, word, and deed.

5. We believe that the Lord Jesus Christ died for our sins according to the Scriptures as a representative and substitutionary sacrifice; and that all who believe in Him are justified on the grounds of His shed blood.

6. We believe in the resurrection of the crucified body of our Lord, in His ascension into Heaven, and in His present life there for us, as High Priest and Advocate.

7. We believe in "that blessed hope," the personal, pre-millennial, and imminent return of our Lord and Savior Jesus Christ.

8. We believe that all who receive by faith the Lord Jesus Christ are born again of the Holy Spirit and thereby become children of God.

9. We believe in the bodily resurrection of the just and the unjust, the everlasting, conscious punishment of the lost.

Fundamentals of Protestantism

1. **Authority of Scripture**--While Protestants are more dogmatic about the absolute authority of Scripture, there is a wide difference of opinion. Most Christians in fundamental Protestant churches rely on the Textus Receptus, or the Majority Text, which supplied eighty-five percent or more of the text for the King James Version of the Bible. Some Christians continue to refuse to accept the newer versions and translations which have relied on the Minority Text and the Westcott and Hort revisions. Increasingly, seminary graduates of liberal schools interpret which scriptures are relative to faith and service and which are what they interpret only the opinions of men.

2. **Creation**--Basic fundamental churches have retained

faith in the Genesis account of creation by a supreme Creator. More liberal churches and theologians have espoused theistic evolution.

3. **The original sin**--Protestant and non-Catholic churches are divided over this basic Christian doctrine. The more fundamental churches believe that since Adam, man is born a sinner and eternally lost without redemption. The more liberal churches believe that man is inherently good with social and environmental conditions responsible for man's moral behavior.

4. **Salvation**--The Calvinistic (not necessarily hard-line predestianism) understanding of salvation is only by and through faith in the atoning, substitutionary, redeeming death of Jesus Christ on the cross, taking the sins of the believer upon Himself and paying the supreme penalty--death, Hell, and the grave. The Calvinistic concept of salvation also entails the security of the believer, the Pauline declaration that the sinner is saved to work; does not work to be saved. About fifty percent of Protestantism accepts the Armenian position, that the sinner is saved by faith but can be lost and go to Hell if he fails to live the life acceptable to God. Some, like the Church of Christ, may teach that there is no way anyone can know if they are saved or lost until the Great White Throne judgment.

5. **Baptism**--Some baptize by sprinkling, some by pouring, some by immersion. Some believe that baptism is an integral part of salvation, and without it there can be no salvation. Some believe that baptism is a declaration to the church of the new Christian's inward faith in the death, burial, and resurrection of Jesus Christ, and an open declaration to live as Jesus Christ would have him or her live before the world. Others

believe that baptism has no relevance to salvation,
church membership, or service.

6. **Communion**--There are also wide variances of beliefs
about the Lord's Supper. Some have closed communion, only administered to members of that particular church. Other churches have open communion, anyone who professes to be a Christian may
participate. Some use wine, some use grape juice.
Some have communion once a year, some every
three months, some once a week.

7. **Trinity**--Some believe that the Godhead is three in
one--Father, Son, and Holy Spirit. Others, like the
Unitarians, believe there is but one God, yet call
themselves Christians. Some profess God the Father,
yet do not honor Jesus Christ as co-equal with the
Father. Some believe the ministry of the Holy Spirit
is to convict the unsaved of sin, upon evidence of faith
in Jesus Christ, give a new birth into the family of
God, and then lead the new Christian into understanding of God's Word. Others concentrate on the
ministry of the Holy Spirit to be miracles, healings,
and speaking in "tongues."

We could continue and list all tenets of Christian
faith and service, but just these seven points should
illustrate the mass confusion and disunity that exists
within Protestant and non-Catholic Christendom. Often, there will be one church across the street from
another church, with the only difference being that one
allows music accompaniment with hymns and the other
does not. I visited my hometown church that I attended
as a youth. This church did not use music; however, a
relative that was the song leader would begin each
hymn by sounding a tuning fork. After the service, this
relative criticized me for belonging to a church that

used musical instruments. The point made was that there is no scripture in the New Testament indicating that such instruments were ever employed in a New Testament church. But I also pointed out to my kinsman that if he would show me a scripture for the tuning fork, I would give him a scripture for our piano and organ. Billions of dollars contributed to the Lord's work, and billions of man-hours in Christian service, are wasted because of duplicating efforts over such silly doctrinal differences. Again, this is another reason why there are so many churches.

To list just the doctrinal differences of the Protestant and non-Catholic churches would run into the thousands and possibly hundreds of thousands, yet each denomination or church will usually stand solidly behind every point of doctrine, teaching, liturgy, and organizational structure. Yet, it seems apparent that if there is but one God, one Savior, one Holy Spirit, and with God there is no variableness, then only one teaching can be true, only one doctrine can be true, and all the others save one is error and not of God.

The Apostle Paul stated in Ephesians 4:3-6, *"Endeavouring to keep the unity of the Spirit in the bond of peace. There is one body, and one Spirit, even as ye are called in one hope of your calling; One Lord, one faith, one baptism, One God and Father of all, who is above all, and through all, and in you all."* Some attempt to explain the baptism referred to in this scripture as "water baptism," but Dr. Kenneth Wuest, the noted Greek scholar, stated:

> *"Why should all the other words be translated and this alone* [hen baptisma] *be transliterated? Why should the A.V. and commentators transliterate the word, interpreting the Greek word as referring to the rite of water baptism when the entire context is*

supernatural, even to the faith exercised by the believer in appropriating salvation? The words translated are 'one placing into.' That is, in response to our act of faith, we were placed by the Holy Spirit into the Body of Christ of which Christ is the Head."

Dr. Wuest contends that the Greek text indicates believers are put into one body by the baptism of the Holy Spirit, not by water baptism. This is consistent with other statements by Paul on the subject: *"For by one Spirit are we all baptized into one body..."* (1 Cor. 12:13).

Are we advocating ecumenism? Definitely yes! Not the political, social, and organizational ecumenism proposed by the Roman Catholic Church, the World Council of Churches, or the National Council of Churches, but rather the unity of believers that Paul prayed could be attained through one common faith in the Lord Jesus Christ.

Chapter Fifteen

New Testament Chronology

A clear teaching in seminaries and churches in regards to the order in which the books of the New Testament are written, why they were written in the order they were, and to whom they were written, doubtless would have prevented to some degree the denominational explosion. Although no infallibility is claimed in the presenting of this New Testament chronology, I believe it is worthy of careful consideration.

Book Number One--A.D. 45, *The General Epistle of James*

This book is the first one in the New Testament to be written. It was written by James, a brother of Jesus Christ, and co-leader of the Jerusalem church with Peter. It was written to "the twelve tribes scattered abroad." From the text of the epistle it can be determined it was written to the Jewish disciples who had been scattered into other nations in the persecution period that followed the stoning of Stephen and the killing of the Apostle James by Herod Agrippa I. From the twenty-first chapter of Acts it can be easily concluded that although the Jewish disciples were faithful to Jesus Christ within the Kingdom gospel committed to Peter, they were diligent in keeping the commandments of the law. Thus, James stressed justification by works and deeds. Ministers and pastors indulge in agonizing doctrinal contortions to try to reconcile justification by faith as taught by Paul with the justification by works in James. Reconciling of the two would be much easier if it is recognized just who wrote this epistle, to whom it is written, when it was written, and why.

Book Number Two--A.D. 54, *The First Epistle of Paul to the Thessalonians*

This book is the first epistle written by Paul and the second book of the New Testament. From the seventeenth chapter of Acts we know that many of the Greeks at Thessalonica believed the gospel that Paul preached and a church was established. However, the Jews threatened Paul's life and he escaped to Athens. Silas and Timothy stayed in the city for a while to help the young church become grounded in the faith. Nevertheless, the new Christians came under heavy persecution. Paul wrote the church this epistle to commend them for their faith, good works, and courage in withstanding the severe attacks in which some had died. Paul encouraged them to in continue the faith of Jesus Christ, because Jesus Christ promised He would return. Paul, rightfully, still expected the Lord to come back, and each chapter in 1 Thessalonians ends with the promise of the coming of the Lord from Heaven to save Christians from the wrath to come. The apostle, in chapter four, verses thirteen through eighteen, assured the brethren at Thessalonica that their loved ones who had already died because of their faith would be raised first. This epistle is the basis for much of the fundamental and pre-millennial doctrine concerning the Rapture of the church.

Book Number Three--A.D. 54, *The Second Epistle of Paul* *to the Thessalonians*

After receiving the first epistle of Paul to them, the Thessalonians continued under extreme persecution, so much so that they thought they must be in the Great Tribulation of which Paul told them must come. In the first chapter, Paul assured these tormented Christians that God would avenge them against their enemies with flaming fire at the Lord's coming. In chapter two Paul admitted their great tribulations, but he again assured them that they could not be in *the* Great Tribulation because the Antichrist had not as yet sat in the Temple of God showing himself as God to all the world. Again Paul encouraged them to *"...stand fast, and hold the traditions which ye have been taught, whether by word, or our epistle"* (1 Thess. 2:15). In chapter three the apostle again exhorted the Thessalonian Christians to be "patient waiting for Christ." This epistle provides insight into the spiritual conditions of the world leading up to the Great Tribulation and the Abomination of Desolation prophesied by Daniel and Jesus Christ.

Book Number Four--A.D. 57, *The First Epistle of Paul to the Corinthians*

Paul lived in Corinth for eighteen months and worked as a tentmaker. Luke reported some of the events of the apostle's ministry in this city in the eighteenth chapter of Acts. Corinth was a large seaport, racially diverse with many languages spoken, wealthy with many sinful temptations. Paul established a large assembly, but after his departure many problems arose. This letter was written to counsel the church leadership in trying to reconcile the problems. The specific issues that Paul offered advice on were: baptism, schisms, fornication and adultery, works in relation to salvation, Christians suing Christians, women's place in the church,

marriage and divorce, faithfulness in church atten-
dance, the Lord's Supper, confusion of languages,
order of resurrection, and Christian stewardship in
giving. This epistle is a very important one in providing
instructions on Christian living, church order, and
service.

Book Number Five--A.D. 57-58, *The Epistle of Paul to the*
Romans

The book of Romans was written to Roman Christians. It is one of the most profound documents to have
ever been conceived in the mind of man in any age.
Although the recipients of this letter were Christians,
they were also Romans; and they were probably having
difficulty reconciling their citizenship in Heaven with
their citizenship in Rome. Roman law was the judicial
force of the known world in the first century; so Paul put
the Jew, the Greek, and the Barbarian (which included
Romans) on trial before the Great Judge. The conclusion was, *"...they are without excuse...there is none*
righteous...there is none that doeth good, no, not one...all have
sinned, and come short of the glory of God." But in the fifth
chapter of Romans, Paul presents news of a pardon for
the guilty by faith in Jesus Christ who died for sinners.
Israel was under domination by Rome, so why should
the Romans believe in a dead Jew or His disciples from
a downtrodden and defeated nation? Paul gives the
answer: *"Hath God cast away his people? God forbid...blindness*
in part is happened to Israel, until the fulness of the Gentiles be
come in. And so all Israel shall be saved....There shall come out
of Sion the Deliverer..." (Rom. 11). Rome ruled the
governments of the world, a matter of intense pride and
arrogance, a stumbling block for many who would
believe in the Kingdom of Jesus Christ. But again Paul
addressed this issue: *"...For there is no power but of God: the*

powers that be are ordained of God" (Rom. 13:1). Romans was written at the proper time to cut through nationalism and open the way for any sinner from any nation to believe in Jesus Christ and be saved.

Book Number Six--A.D. 58, *The Second Epistle of Paul to the Corinthians*

Paul's second letter to the church at Corinth was written for a number of reasons, but nothing actually specific. At the time of the writing of the epistle, Paul was in Philippi in upper Greece, or Macedonia. He first tells them about the extreme dangers he faced at Ephesus and thanked them for their prayers. The apostle then explains why he was not able to come to them in person as promised. Evidently some had questioned Paul's honesty in using the offerings taken for the saints and new questions about his apostleship had arisen. Paul defended himself against these charges and then warned the church to beware of false teachers. In closing, Paul exhorts those who had not repented of their sinful and worldly ways to do so; because, when he would be able to see them in person, he would deal with them severely. Paul's second letter to the Corinthian Christians is a warm and beautiful letter because the apostle discusses many personal things about himself as well as the things of a personal concern to the members of that church, teaching us that God is indeed interested in us in a personal way.

Book Number Seven--A.D. 58, *The Epistle of Paul to the Galatians*

Some commentaries date this letter of Paul to A.D. 54 or 55, but it appears more evident from the book of Acts it was written several years later. The reason for the letter is conclusive from the very text itself. There are some troublesome aspects of this letter which most ministers either overlook or are afraid to discuss. It is obvious that disciples from the church at Jerusalem, perhaps Pharisees who had professed Jesus Christ, had infiltrated the churches of Galatia, teaching that Gentile Christians must be circumcised, thus brought under the commandments of the law. Paul goes to great length to protest that his gospel, whereby the Galatian Christians had been converted to Christ, was not taught him, nor did he receive it from any of the leaders or members of the church at Jerusalem, including Peter, James, or John. He also goes into much detail to show that Peter's gospel of the Circumcision was not to be preached to the Uncircumcision, or Gentiles. Paul does not definitely say that these false teachers were sent by the church at Jerusalem, but he does make the connection. The message of Galatians is, *"But though we, or an angel from heaven, preach any other gospel unto you than that which we have preached unto you, let him be accursed"* (Gal. 1:8). Although Paul seemed to believe that the Galatian church had been corrupted almost beyond redemption, he held out hope for a few: *"And as many as walk according to this rule, peace be on them, and mercy, and upon the Israel of God"* (Gal. 6:16). This epistle needs to be taught, verse by verse, in every Christian church in the world.

Book Number Eight--A.D. 61, *The Gospel According to Matthew*

The Apostle Paul returned to Israel although warned by the Holy Spirit to continue his ministry to the Gentiles. Paul was not successful in bringing about a repentance in Israel so that Jesus would return. The apostle was arrested for his own protection, confined in a Roman jail in Caesarea for two years, and then sent to

Rome at his own request. Shortly after Paul arrived in Rome, Matthew wrote the first of the gospels to appear in writing. Some sources place the time of writing from A.D. 69 to 85. Scholars who worked on the notes of the Oxford Pilgrim Edition of the Bible, as well as the Scofield Bible, agree that the date was A.D. 61 and no later than A.D. 62. Had Jesus Christ returned as a result of the ministry of the Jerusalem church under the leadership of Peter, John, and James, there would have been no need for the gospels, because the Living Word would rule on earth. But with the arrest and imprisonment of Paul in Rome, when hope of repentance and an acceptance of Jesus Christ as the Messiah grew even more remote, the first record of the birth, ministry, death, resurrection, and ascension of the Savior appeared. The man who wrote it was Matthew, an apostle, who gave personal testimony to what he had seen and heard. The gospel according to Matthew presents Jesus Christ, the Messiah and rightful heir to the throne of David. The genealogy of Jesus is traced in Jewish history back to Abraham, proving that He had a right to David's throne. King Herod, an Edomite, renewed the controversy between the house of Jacob and the house of Esau as prophesied. The birthplace of Jesus and His miracles were foretold in the Old Testament. Therefore, the message of the gospel according to Matthew was: the promised Messiah has come; the King is here; repent and get ready for the Kingdom is at hand. The messianic message to Israel by Jesus was, "...*I am not sent but unto the lost sheep of the house of Israel*" (Matt. 15:24). In the prophecies of Jesus recorded by Matthew, especially in the Olivet Discourse, the second coming of Jesus Christ to ultimately bring in the Kingdom is recorded. In the so-called Great Commission (Matt. 28:18-20), Matthew presents Jesus as committing to the

Jewish disciples the message of the Kingdom, which was to teach to the nations. The Gentile church age is not in view in Matthew.

Book Number Nine--A.D. 61, *The Gospel According to Luke*

It is the general consensus that the sixty-six books of the Bible were written by forty Jews over a period of sixteen hundred years. However, some believe that one of the writers, Luke, was not a Jew. Others favor the opinion that Luke was a Grecian Jew. The earliest date given for the writing of this gospel is A.D. 61; other dates range from A.D. 63 to 90. There is no evidence in Luke's gospel or Acts that he ever saw Jesus Christ, although he could have. It appears that his gospel account was collected from other sources. Luke, being a physician, is more detailed in describing births, conception, illnesses, and healings. There is much difference between the gospel of Luke and the gospel of Matthew. An entire volume would be required to analyze the variations. Luke's gospel is less Jewish centered, flowing in more of a Gentile style of expression, and more Gentile and worldwide in scope. Luke gives the genealogy back to Adam, making Jesus Christ the Creator and Lord of all humanity, not just of the Jews. Phrases strictly limiting the ministry of Jesus to Israel are absent. Matthew points to the fig tree budding (Israel) as a sign of the end of the age; Luke has Jesus pointing to the fig tree and all the trees (all nations). Another sign of the end within the Olivet Discourse in the twenty-first chapter of Luke is the fulfillment of the times of the Gentiles. This sign is omitted in Matthew. While Matthew indicates the Great Commission is given to Jewish disciples to proclaim, Luke simply says it is to be preached. Luke also has Jesus pointing to Pentecost;

Matthew does not. It seems reasonable that after the Jews rejected the testimony of Paul, sought to kill him, and the apostle was put in prison, Luke could have written the account of the life, ministry, and resurrection of Jesus as it would apply to all the world. The writing of the gospel according to Luke could have been as early as A.D. 59.

Book Number Ten--A.D. 61, *The Acts of the Apostles*
This book by Luke was also addressed to Theophilus, which means "lover of God." Whether Theophilus was an actual friend or Luke was writing to everyone who loves God is a matter of opinion. The first fifteen chapters of Acts were written from accounts told to Luke by others, as Luke did not join Paul until Acts 16:10 where the noun form changes from "they" and "them" to "we." Luke must have gotten much of his information about the early church from Barnabas, Silas, or Mark. Paul provided information about the events of chapters ten through fifteen, and the apostle refers to many of those events in his epistles. The historical pattern of Acts is to emphasize the early church and the gospel of the Circumcision in the first ten chapters, and then changes in emphasis to the Pauline revelation which Paul was committed to preach to the Gentiles. It is assumed that Acts was written as a diary between A.D. 52 and 61. The closing verses of Acts concern Paul's last attempt to witness to a delegation of Jews in Rome. When they departed without reaching a conclusion concerning Jesus Christ as the Messiah, Paul declared, *"For the heart of this people is waxed gross, and their ears are dull of hearing, and their eyes have they closed; lest they should see with their eyes, and hear with their ears, and understand with their heart, and should be converted, and I should heal them. Be it known therefore unto you, that the*

salvation of God is sent unto the Gentiles, and that they will hear it" (Acts 28:27-28). There is an association of independent churches, often referred to as hyperdispensationalists, who believe that only the epistles written by Paul after Acts 28:28 are meant for the church. It is apparent that after Acts 28:28 Paul felt no leading of the Holy Spirit to preach Jesus Christ according to the covenants to the Jews first. On the other hand, Paul makes no mention of receiving a second revelation of the Gospel to preach to the Gentiles. It is our belief that all of Paul's epistles are for Gentile salvation, growth, and service, with some parts of the pre-prison epistles (Romans, Galatians, 1 Corinthians, 2 Corinthians, 1 Thessalonians, 2 Thessalonians) having reference to preach Jesus Christ to the Jews from the messianic promises as he was committed to do. After Acts 28:28, this obligation ceased.

Book Number Eleven--A.D. 62, *The Epistle of Paul to the Ephesians*

That Paul was in prison when he wrote this epistle is evident, as he makes two references to being a prisoner. This epistle constitutes a basic statement of faith by Paul for the Gentile churches:

1. Christians are the adopted children of God through faith in Jesus Christ.
2. Salvation is sealed by the Holy Spirit until the day of redemption.
3. The destination of Christians is heavenly, not earthly.
4. Christians are saved by grace through faith in Jesus Christ.
5. Salvation is by faith; works are to follow.
6. Christians are not obligated to keep the ordinances and commandments to Israel except in love.

7. The authority of the revelation of Paul to preach to the Gentiles apart from any other authority.
8. The unity of faith in the Gospel preached by Paul.
9. Grieve not the Holy Ghost, live not in sinful lusts.
10. Strengthen family relationships.
11. Remain strong in the faith and resist satanic deceptions and evil spirits.

Book Number Twelve--A.D. 62, *The Epistle of Paul to the Colossians*

The city of Colosse was located in an area of southern Galatia adjacent to Asia. Paul is mentioned in the sixteenth chapter of Acts as having passed through the area, but evidently did not stop at Colosse or Laodicea. The churches in these cities were founded by other Christians, but Paul established his authority to instruct them in chapter one: *"...I am made a minister, according to the dispensation of God which is given to me for you, to fulfil the word of God; Even the mystery which hath been hid from ages and from generations..."* (Col. 1:25-26). In the epistle, Paul presents sound Christian doctrine for faith, service, and living before the world, covering again the tenets of faith presented in his epistle to the Ephesians. However, as it was in the churches of Galatia, false teachers were attempting to subvert the Christians by bringing them back under the law. There is also evidence in the epistle that even the teaching of the Essenes was troubling some. Paul refers to his prison bonds and that Luke was still with him at the time. The apostle instructs that this letter be read in the other churches of Phrygia that needed the same instructions.

Book Number Thirteen--A.D. 62, *The Epistle of Paul to Philemon*

Philemon was a wealthy land owner who lived at

Colosse, or some other city in southern Asia or Galatia. He evidently was a prominent Christian as his house was a church meeting place. At that time, according to Gibbons, half of the Roman Empire was bonded slaves, either through captivity or the poor selling themselves into bondage. Onesimus, a slave of Philemon, had run away, taking with him some of the master's money, a crime punishable by death. Paul, through the Gospel, led him to a saving faith in Jesus Christ. In Colossian 4:9 Onesimus is referred to by Paul as "a faithful and beloved brother." Paul's letter to Philemon in behalf of Onesimus is a type of the intercession that Jesus Christ makes for all Christians before the throne of the Father. Ephesians, Colossians, and Philemon were all written at one time, and Onesimus and Tychicus travelled together as they sailed back to Asia. Onesimus took his letter to Philemon, and Tychicus delivered Paul's letters to the churches at Ephesus and Colosse.

Book Number Fourteen--A.D. 63, *The Epistle of Paul to the Philippians*

The main reason for this epistle was to thank the church at Philippi for their generous offering to help the apostle during his time of imprisonment. The offering was sent by Epaphroditus who had fallen ill in Rome, but upon recovering took the letter back to the church. Paul also acknowledges the generosity of the church in assisting with offerings on former occasions. At the time of the writing of this epistle, nothing is mentioned about Mark and Luke; however, Timothy was with Paul. Mention is made of the saints in Caesar's household, indicating that many of those in the Roman government had been won to faith in Jesus Christ. Paul and Silas had been imprisoned in Philippi and the apostle established a church in this city which is about one hundred miles east of Thessalonica on the coast of the Aegean Sea (Acts 16). This epistle is perhaps the most positive and joyful of all the Pauline letters, perhaps because Paul was expecting to be released soon from prison and even to visit the brethren at Philippi in person (2:19-24). Paul expresses his joy in giving up all things of the world in exchange for salvation in Jesus Christ. He encouraged the members of the church to keep a positive attitude, to live at peace with God and man, and to live by faith in God, putting no confidence in the flesh. He concludes the letter with an uplifting promise: *"But my God shall supply all your need according to his riches in glory by Jesus Christ"* (Phil. 4:19). Even at the late date of A.D. 63, Paul was still looking for the return of Jesus Christ in his lifetime (3:15-21). Paul's epistle to the church at Philippi is most important in teaching Christians the way to live the overcoming life in Jesus Christ before the world.

Book Number Fifteen--A.D. 63, *The First Epistle of Peter*
    The writer of this epistle is identified as Peter, the apostle of Jesus Christ. It was written to the strangers, evidently meaning Jewish disciples, who were scattered throughout Asia Minor. As far as salvation through faith in Jesus Christ, godly family life, marital relationships, patience in persecutions, spiritual gifts, vigilance against Satan, maintaining a righteous testimony before the world, Peter seems to touch all the bases. And there is no mention of being circumcised, obeying the law of Moses for righteousness, or offering sacrifices for sin as was observed by the church at Jerusalem in A.D. 58 (see Acts 21). Peter mentions the Gentiles who were ungodly. He also makes an indirect reference to Gentile Christians who *"...in time past were not a people, but are now*

the people of God: which had not obtained mercy, but now have obtained mercy" (1 Pet. 2:10). There is no indication in the epistle that Peter attempts to minister to Gentile Christians; be mindful that his gospel was for the Circumcision. Mark was evidently with Peter when this epistle was written. Mark had been with Paul in Rome in A.D. 62 when the letter was written to Philemon, but in A.D. 63 he is with Peter. Note should also be taken that Paul did not mention Mark when he wrote the epistle to the Philippians in A.D. 63. Evidently Mark left Paul and joined Peter. The first epistle of Peter was written from Babylon, and while in the second and third centuries Christians thought of Rome as Mystery Babylon, the Babylon of this epistle was probably the Babylon on the Euphrates. Many of the Jews stayed in Babylon, and at the time of Jesus Christ, there was still a large population of Jews in a new city adjacent to the old Babylon. There is no evidence that Peter was ever in Rome, regardless of the attempt by Roman Catholicism to make Peter the first pope. Had Peter been in Rome, Paul would surely have mentioned his presence. The person who did the actual writing was Silas. The last known whereabouts of Silas were in Corinth with Paul five years earlier. This may account for why parts of this epistle sound as much like Paul as Peter. The reference to "judgment must begin at the house of God" may have a double meaning. The only house of God in the Bible in reference to an actual building was the Temple in Jerusalem. Peter may have realized that the prophecy of Jesus that the Temple would be destroyed in that generation was at hand.

Book Number Sixteen--A.D. 63-64, *The Epistle of Paul to the Hebrews*

The Oxford Pilgrim Edition of the Bible names

Paul as the author of Hebrews. Other sources have named Luke as the author, and still others say the author cannot be determined. From Philippians we know that in A.D. 63 Paul was expected to be released from prison, and in connection with this thought we refer to Hebrews 13:23, *"Know ye not that our brother Timothy is set at liberty; with whom, if he come shortly, I will see you."* If the author was Paul, then naturally he would have waited for Timothy to get out of prison also before leaving Italy. When Paul was in Jerusalem in A.D. 58, he found the church under the leadership of James still worshipping in the Temple, keeping the law, and offering up sacrifices for committed sins. Hebrews was written to Jewish disciples at Jerusalem, and the subject is keeping the law for righteousness, accepting the high priest as mediator, and continuing sacrificial worship at the Temple. Also, Paul was considered a traitor by the Jews and a blasphemer by some in the Jerusalem church. Therefore, again, if Paul was the author, then there would be good reason for not identifying himself. There are many wonderful truths in Hebrews, but many pastors and laymen have great trouble in misapplying them. In studying Hebrews it should be kept in mind that this epistle was not written to Gentile Christians, but Jewish disciples at Jerusalem who had an even greater backsliding problem than the churches of Galatia. In our opinion, it was written by Paul in late A.D. 63 or early A.D. 64. The scribe was probably Timothy.

Book Number Seventeen--late A.D. 64 or early A.D. 65, *The First Epistle of Paul to Timothy*

After Paul was released from prison along with Timothy, it is thought that they took a ship to Asia. Paul left Timothy to assume pastoral duties over the church at Ephesus while he travelled on to Philippi in Macedonia, as he had previously expressed intentions to do. Other historical notes indicate that this epistle was written by Paul from Laodicea, the principal city of the province of Phrygia. Still other sources indicate it was written from Corinth. In any event, this letter is the first of the three pastoral epistles written by Paul. It contains specific instructions for church government and pastoral responsibility, as well as many pitfalls to avoid. In the first chapter Timothy is cautioned to be on guard against false teachers who preach salvation by works rather than by faith in Jesus Christ (vs. 19). Chapter two concerns instructions to the pastor about the importance of prayer, modesty in women's dress, keeping church leadership under man's authority, and restates his authority as an apostle to the Gentiles (vs. 7). Chapter three lists the qualifications for bishops and deacons. Chapter four presents another strong warning to be on guard against false teachers, especially those who forbid marriage and abstinence from eating meat. Chapter five gives advice to the pastor or a bishop in conducting himself before the membership with elders, young men, children of the brethren, widows and young women. Paul also advises Timothy about his right to receive a salary; and, if wrongs are committed openly then they should be discussed openly before the congregation. Chapter six relates to spiritual harmony between master and slave, and the rich and the poor. Another warning concerns unscriptural tales and false science. Although Paul's hope in the return of Jesus in his lifetime had doubtless waned, he still held out this hope: *"...thou keep this commandment without spot, unrebukeable, until the appearing of our Lord Jesus Christ"* (1 Tim. 6:14). This epistle remains an excellent guide for proper church government.

Book Number Eighteen--A.D. 64 or early A.D. 65, *The Epistle of Paul to Titus*

Titus was a Gentile. He is mentioned several times as being a fellow missionary with Paul and a valuable servant of the Lord Jesus Christ. From what records that are available, it appears that Paul, after leaving Timothy at Ephesus, picked up Titus. After travelling through Asia, he went to Philippi and then to Corinth. From Corinth, Paul sent Titus to take charge of the churches at Crete. The Cretians were a mixed race with no respect for governmental authority. According to Paul's own accusations, they were lazy, liars, drunkards, thieves, and immoral. Many would profess Jesus Christ for gain when they had no faith at all (3:16). As if Titus did not have enough trouble with the Cretians, *"...there are many unruly and vain talkers and deceivers, specially they of the circumcision: Whose mouths must be stopped, who subvert whole houses, teaching things which they ought not, for filthy lucre's sake"* (Titus 1:10-11). Paul informed Titus that often in such ungodly situations, pastors and missionaries must be realistic and establish order out of chaos before God's Holy Spirit can save souls.

Book Number Nineteen--A.D. 66, *The General Epistle of Jude*

The author of this brief epistle was Jude (Judas--not Judas Iscariot), the brother of James, and one of the brothers of Jesus Christ. The date of its writing is somewhat uncertain. Historic evidence would indicate it was written before the destruction of the Temple and Jerusalem in A.D. 70, and verses seventeen and eighteen indicate that it was written before Peter wrote his second epistle. Thus, the year A.D. 66 is a reasonable conclusion. Verses fourteen and fifteen were taken from the Book of Enoch, a book not considered inspired of God. Verse nine is also from a dubious source, and this epistle was not included in the canons until A.D. 367. Jude warns against the great increase in false teachers, thus it was put next to Revelation as giving an important sign of the last days as Jesus prophesied. Paul wrote in 1 Corinthians 9:5 that the brethren of Jesus had wives, doubtless including James and Jude. According to Eusebius, two grandsons of Jude were taken to Emperor Domitian with charges that they were descendants of King David and rightful heirs to the throne of Israel. Domitian dismissed them as harmless peasants. The book is not addressed particularly to Jewish disciples, and it is not known if it was circulated in the first century Gentile churches. It did receive wide attention in the second century. The only doctrinal issue of consequence in Jude is verse twelve, where it is inferred that those who knowingly acknowledge Jesus Christ as Lord, but turn against Him and commit damnable heresies to deceive others have made their choice and have no hope of salvation. They are twice dead according to a literal reading of this scripture. The epistle of Jude constitutes a warning to the church of Satan's plan to divide and conquer. In considering the multitude of denominations and cults, it is evident the Devil has not changed his plan because it works over and over again.

Book Number Twenty--A.D. 66, *The Second Epistle of Peter*

Some sources date the writings of this epistle to A.D. 68 or 69. Others, because of cross references in Jude, date it as early as A.D. 66. Since Paul's confrontation with Peter at Antioch, Peter appears to have confined his ministry to the Circumcision. However, whereas his first epistle was written to Jewish disciples, his second is addressed to "them that have obtained like precious faith." This could mean that Paul had already been executed in Rome, or it could mean that Peter had reconciled his gospel to the Circumcision with Paul's gospel to the Uncircumcision as indicated in 2 Peter 3:15-16: *"And account that the longsuffering of our Lord is salvation; even as our beloved brother Paul also according to the wisdom given unto him hath written unto you; As also in all his epistles, speaking in them of these things; in which are some things hard to be understood, which they that are unlearned and unstable wrest, as they do also the other scriptures, unto their own destruction."* Peter admits that some of Paul's gospel is hard to understand and even his paraphrasing of Paul's statements on salvation leaves something to be desired. It is uncertain where Peter was when he wrote this epistle. It appeared early in Jewish Christian circles, but it was slow to be accepted by Gentile churches. The message to Christians is to make their calling and election "sure" (1:10). Peter seems to say that good works and Christian growth should follow salvation as evidence that the foundation of salvation in Christ has really been laid. In chapter one Peter mentioned his approaching death as Jesus Christ foretold, martyrdom by crucifixion. Some traditions indicate that Peter asked to be crucified with his head down, not feeling worthy to be crucified in the same manner as Jesus. Peter was not a Roman citizen so he was not entitled to a hearing in Rome. He could have been executed anywhere in the Roman Empire. In chapter one Peter speaks of his being with Jesus on the Mount of Transfiguration and encourages Christians to study prophecy relating to the Lord's return. Chapter two is a stinging indictment against false teachers, and as the epistle of Jude and the tenth chapter of Hebrews infers, knowledge that Jesus Christ is Messiah, Savior, and Lord is not enough. If a person comes to the knowledge of this truth, but then does not accept it and teaches others to disbelieve it, their *"...latter end is worse with them than the beginning. For it had been better for them not to have known the way of righteousness."* Chapter three contains a warning against mockers who, in the last days, would deny signs of the Lord's return. Christians are exhorted to win souls as the day of the Lord is at hand (3:9), as well as being steadfast and faithful as that day approaches. Because so much of Peter's second epistle has a setting in the end-time, it is a particularly appropriate book for church study today.

Book Number Twenty-One--A.D. 67, *The Second Epistle of Paul to Timothy*

A Roman citizen convicted of a crime had a right to appeal to Caesar. Paul was released from prison by Nero in A.D. 64, but he was arrested again on another crime in late A.D. 66 and sent back to Rome. It was at this time that Nero blamed his problems and the burning of Rome on the Christians. It was from prison in Rome that Paul wrote his last epistle, which was his second epistle to Timothy. The opening verses constitute a personal greeting to Timothy, with an exhortation to be true in preaching the *"...gospel according to the power of God;* **Who hath saved us....**" In the first chapter, knowing that he is to be executed soon, Paul affirms again his right to be an apostle, God's appointed preacher and teacher to the Gentiles (1:10-12). Paul also makes mention, evidently, about his recent journey to the churches he had established and visited previously: *"This thou knowest, that all they which are in Asia be turned away from me...."* It is apparent that false teachers and prophets had perverted the simple gospel of grace in most of the churches in both Galatia and Asia. Throughout this epistle, Paul seems to have crowded as much

Gospel truth as possible, knowing that this would be his last effort:

> *"...for I know whom I have believed, and am persuaded that he is able to keep that which I have committed unto him against that day"* (1:12).

> *"It is a faithful saying: For if we be dead with him, we shall also live with him: If we suffer, we shall also reign with him: if we deny him, he also will deny us"* (2:11-12).

> *"Study to shew thyself approved unto God, a workman that needeth not to be ashamed, rightly dividing the word of truth"* (2:15).

> *"All scripture is given by inspiration of God, and is profitable for doctrine, for reproof, for correction, for instruction in righteousness: That the man of God may be perfect, throughly furnished unto all good works"* (3:16-17).

> *"Preach the word; be instant in season, out of season; reprove, rebuke, exhort with all long-suffering and doctrine"* (4:2).

> *"...I am now ready to be offered, and the time of my departure is at hand. I have fought a good fight, I have finished my course, I have kept the faith"* (4:6-7).

In chapter three Paul warns of perilous times that will come in the last days, the most prominent being the breakup of the home and the discarding of godly family values. Chapter four is a final charge to Timothy to be faithful to preach the Gospel, which Paul refers to as "my gospel" (2:8). With his last few words in the epistle he made a reference to the second coming, *"Henceforth there is laid up for me a crown of righteousness, which the Lord, the righteous judge, shall give me at that day: and not to me only, but unto all them also that love his appearing"* (4:8). The *Fausett Dictionary and Encyclopedia* (p. 550) quotes reliable historical sources to the effect that Peter was crucified in Babylon (did not go to Rome) and Paul died by the sword (probably beheading) on the Ostian Way. Death would have been by order of Nero. One historian gives the year as A.D. 67; another as A.D. 68. Fausett adds:

> *"The apocryphal 'Clemtines' at the end of the second century contain a curious attack on his* [Paul's] *authority and exaltation of Peter and James. It is a rising of the old judaical leaven, impatient of the Gospel anti-legalism of Paul."*

Again we see from the earliest church history to the present time it is the mixing of the ministry of Peter and the ministry of Paul that has caused confusion and division. For doctrinal reasons, some even moved the execution site of Peter to Rome. Constantine erected a monument at the site of Paul's execution, but it was not Paul's death that was important, but his life dedicated to the calling out of this world from the Gentiles a people for Christ's Name.

Book Number Twenty-Two--A.D. 67, *The Gospel According to Mark*

John Mark, called Marcus by the Romans, was a young man at the time of the crucifixion of Jesus. It is not known if he ever saw Jesus, but it is probable that

Mark was the young man mentioned in Mark 14:51-52 who fled naked from the scene. This incident is mentioned in no other book of the Bible; it would have importance only to Mark. However, the evident fact that Mark had to depend upon Peter for many details about the ministry of Jesus would indicate that he was not an active disciple. Peter went to the house of Mary, the mother of Mark, after he was delivered from prison (Acts 12, A.D. 45). Paul and Barnabas took young Mark (probably about twenty-five years old at the time) with them on their first missionary journey. Mark evidently became homesick and left them. Paul refused to take Mark with him again. However, Mark continued to go on missions with Barnabas and Peter. In the late fifties the Apostle Paul acknowledged that this disciple had matured and become quite profitable to him. In A.D. 67, Paul requested that Timothy bring Mark to Rome (Peter may have possibly already been crucified). We may wonder why Paul made this request as he did not have long to live. The reason may have been to have Mark write a third account of the life and ministry of Jesus. It is generally agreed by all commentaries that Mark wrote his gospel in Rome in the Greek language, taking out many of the references in Matthew that would be derogatory of the Gentiles. Some scholars concluded that Mark wrote his gospel for the Romans as a testimony, realizing that the church in Rome was soon to come under heavy persecution and martyrdom. Mark, though not an outstanding teacher or preacher, was a servant to those who were. The word *euthus*, translated "immediately," "forthwith," or "straightway," is found forty times in his book. Mark would have heard this word over and over in his lifetime, being a servant to the apostles. So in his gospel, Mark stresses the ministry of Jesus, not only as King, Lord, and

Savior, but also as the Suffering Servant to humanity. Mark is more specific than any of the other three writers of the gospels in quoting Jesus about the Great Commission. Mark includes *"signs...cast out devils...speak with new tongues...take up serpents...drink any deadly thing...lay hands on the sick."* On the day of Pentecost the disciples did speak with other tongues (languages), Paul cast out demons (Acts 16:18), suffered no ill effects when bitten by a poisonous snake (Acts 28:3), and he healed the sick by laying on of his hand (Acts 28:8). However, Peter, from whom Mark must have received much information about the ministry of Jesus, mentions none of these signs as being evident among the disciples in either of his two epistles. Also, none of these signs or miracles are mentioned by Paul in his prison epistles to the Gentiles. This fact is further evidence that these were signs to Israel and passed away with the demise of the apostles. It is possible that the 144,000 Jewish witnesses of the Lord will be given power to perform these miracles during the Tribulation just prior to the second coming of Jesus Christ.

Book Number Twenty-Three--A.D. 90, *The Gospel According to John*

The most common date given for the writing of this book is A.D. 90, although the exact date cannot be determined. It would appear evident, however, that it was written several years after the destruction of Jerusalem and the Temple by the Romans. Statements like the one in John 1:11-12 are not found in the other gospels: *"He came unto his own, and his own received him not. But as many as received him, to them gave he power to become the sons of God, even to them that believe on his name."* Neither is the gospel call of John 3:16 found in the other gospels: *"For God so loved the world, that he gave his only begotten Son, that whosoever believeth in him should not perish, but have everlasting life."* John leaves out the genealogy of Jesus Christ and most of the incidents and teachings of the Lord that related to the Kingdom promises to Israel. The message of John the Baptist, Jesus, and the apostles to Israel was: Repent, for the Kingdom of Heaven is at hand. The word "repent" is not found in the entire gospel of John. The love of God for lost humanity and salvation through faith in Jesus Christ is the theme of this gospel. The Great Commission is shortened in the last chapter to simply "feed my sheep." It is our understanding that the Holy Spirit led John to write this epistle as a door to open the way for the acceptance of the epistles of Paul. Without the gospel of John, the Pauline revelation would have come under even greater attack than it has. In the gospel of John we see evidence that the Kingdom promise to Israel had been set aside when it was written. The Olivet Discourse in which Jesus foretold the destruction of the Temple is not included in the gospel according to John, possibly because when it was written this particular prophecy had already come to pass. And while the other prophecies of Jesus concerning the last days are also omitted, there is a profound prophetic teaching in the last chapter of this book. At the beginning of the ministry of Jesus on earth, He instructed the disciples to cast their nets on the right side in order to catch fish. The net broke (Luke 5:6), possibly indicating the Kingdom was not to be brought in at this time. After the resurrection of Jesus, He appeared to the disciples and again instructed the disciples to cast their nets on the right side. This time the net did not break and they brought to land one hundred fifty-three huge fish. There are thirteen references in the Bible comparing nations being brought into the Millennial Kingdom to a fisherman catching fish in the net. This teaching of the one hundred fifty-three fish indicates that there will be one hundred fifty-three nations on earth when Jesus Christ returns. God determined seventy nations after the grandsons of Noah, but according to the second chapter of Daniel, at the end of the age the Roman colonial system would be broken up into many nations. This happened after World War II. In John 21:9 the apostle said there was a fish on the fire as the net was being brought to land. During the Great Tribulation, Israel will be the fish on the fire (Zech. 13:8-9). John was the apostle whom Jesus loved, and he was chosen to write this gospel to declare the love of God for all men and the depths of His love in sending His only begotten Son to die for the sins of the world. John also reports the prophecy of Jesus concerning the death of Peter, and that John himself would live longer than any of the other apostles.

Book Number Twenty-Four--A.D. 90, *The First Epistle of John*

It is thought by most biblical chronologists that this epistle was written within the same time frame as John's gospel was written. The writer of this epistle is identified as one who saw Jesus, heard Jesus, and touched Jesus; so there is no reason to believe that the writer is anyone but John. While Paul was alive, John did not infringe upon his calling to preach to the Gentiles. And while John does not mention Paul, this epistle is in doctrinal accord with the Pauline revelation. The epistle is general, meaning to both Jewish believers and Gentile believers alike. The purpose for it, as indicated by John, is explained in the fourth verse of chapter one: *"And these things write we unto you, that your joy may be full."* John explained to Christians how to live the overcoming, victorious life in Christ with specific exhortations to love one another. The apostle also warns against false christs and antichrists who deny that Jesus the Christ had come in the flesh to die for all who would believe. One of the more profound doctrinal truths stated in this epistle is found in 1 John 3:2, *"Beloved, now are we the sons of God...."* Adam was a son of God by direct creation; angels are called sons of God because they were also direct creations. In the Old Testament there is one reference to Israel becoming the sons of God in the Kingdom age, but there was no son of God from Adam to Jesus Christ within mankind. Those looking forward in faith to the coming Messiah waited in Paradise until their sins were atoned for by One who could offer an acceptable sacrifice. But John writes in this epistle that now Christians are "sons of God," born again by faith through the New Birth into the family of God. Like Paul, John preached in his gospel and epistles that salvation was by faith in Jesus Christ. The conclusion that "now" we are the sons of God verifies the eternal security of each believer. However, because Christians are sons of God, John exhorts believers to live above the things of the world and do those things pleasing in God's will. In the concluding chapter, John writes that those born of God, the sons of God by faith, will not live in a condition of sin. Love of God and love for fellow Christians is mentioned fifty times in this epistle. It is thought that John's ministry after the destruction of Jerusalem was centered in the church at Ephesus. The church of St. John, near the Ephesus excavations, dates to the third century and the foundation and parts of the structure are still in evidence. The baptistry in the floor is in the shape of a cross. Also, Jesus committed His mother Mary to John's care, and a tomb said to be the place where Mary was buried is near the church. There is nothing in the first epistle of John that is contrary to the gospel that Paul received from Jesus Christ to preach to the Gentiles.

Book Number Twenty-Five--A.D. 90, *The Second Epistle of John*

This epistle was probably written from Ephesus in A.D. 90, or thereabouts. It was written to the "elect lady" from "the elder." John was an elder in the church at Ephesus. The word for "lady" in the Greek is *kuria*, the root word for *kuriake,* meaning "church." It is thought by many that the epistle was written from Ephesus to the church at Babylon. Early church fathers in their writings stated that John's tomb was at Ephesus. Although brief, this second epistle is much like the first, stressing love as being a new commandment from God to the church, and keeping the commandments or instructions to the churches as evidence of salvation. And, as indicated in his first epistle, Christians need to live in Jesus Christ, above reproach before the world, and thereby receive a full reward. John also warned the membership not to offer fellowship to any who would preach any other doctrine, because they would become as guilty before God as the antichrists, or the false teachers. In closing John expressed hope that he would soon be able to visit the church to whom he addressed this epistle, but there is no evidence that it did, or did not, happen.

Book Number Twenty-Six--A.D. 90, *The Third Epistle of John*

This epistle was written to a prominent church leader named Gaius. Romans was written by Paul while at Corinth residing in the house of Gaius (Rom. 16:23). Gaius was also one of the few at Corinth whom Paul baptized (1 Cor. 1:14). Whether John ever visited Gaius as planned is not known. From this epistle written thirty years after Paul's letters to the church at Corinth, it appears that strife continued within the assembly. While Gaius continued to show much charity toward the saints (evidently Jewish disciples) a man by the name of Diotrephas, by this time, had gained control. Not only would Diotrephas not offer fellowship to John, he threw the brethren (evidently from Ephesus) out of the church. John indicated that when he would go to Corinth he would settle his account with this person. Whether the Gentiles mentioned in verse seven were unbelievers or Gentile Christians is not clear. In any event, as the Apostle John wrote in this epistle, many church divisions had been caused simply by one man, or a group of men, using the church to gain position and power.

Book Number Twenty-Seven--A.D. 96, *The Revelation of Saint John*

This book is misnamed, because in the first verse we read, "The Revelation of Jesus Christ." It was given to John by an angel (vs. 1). The writer of the book identifies himself as John, the same John who wrote the book we know as the gospel according to John. The setting of this book is established in Revelation 1:7: *"Behold, he cometh with clouds; and every eye shall see him, and they also which pierced him: and all kindreds of the earth shall wail because of him. Even so, Amen."* In verse ten of chapter one John wrote that when he received this book from the Lord, he was "in the Spirit on the Lord's day." Many interpret this to mean that John was worshipping on Sunday, the first day of the week. The early church did come to call Sunday the Lord's day, but biblically, the Lord's Day, or the Day of the Lord, always refers to the Tribulation period. Therefore, a better explanation would seem to be that John was translated in the Spirit into the Tribulation and recorded those things he saw which much come to pass. The first chapter describes the actual giver of the Revelation, the eternal Creator, Jesus Christ, the First and the Last. Chapters two and three contain letters to seven churches in Asia Minor. The most common interpretation of the letters is that

1. they were actual churches in these cities in A.D. 96;
2. conditions in these churches represent the types of churches that are in the world; and/or
3. they represent in general seven stages of the church from the first century until the second coming of Jesus Christ.

The letters to the seven churches should not be understood as applying to individual members, except as indicated. Generally, these letters are to be understood as applying to the church as an organization. The language is neither Pauline nor that of the Apostle John in his gospel or epistles. Regardless, these letters reveal the divisions, apostasies, worldliness, false doctrines, and ungodly leaders within the church. A composite description of all these letters would seemingly describe the overall condition of Christendom today. Between Revelation 3 and Revelation 22, the words "church," "churches," or "Christians" are not found. The premillennial, pre-Tribulation explanation is that the church is raptured just prior to the Great Tribulation. In chapters four through nineteen, the Temple is spoken of, Jerusalem is referred to, and likewise the twelve tribes, Israelites, Moses, and Elijah, but not the Gentile church. Also, in these same chapters the judgment of God upon an ungodly, rebellious world are described. These judgments are to culminate at the Battle of

Armageddon, with the Lord Jesus Christ returning to bring in His Kingdom, a thousand years of ruling the nations with a rod of iron. Chapter twenty describes the Millennium, including the Great White Throne judgment, concerning the resurrection and judgment of the lost dead of all ages. Chapters twenty-one and twenty-two describe the New Heaven and the New Earth in which the redeemed of all ages will live, the fulfillment of God's eternal plan and purpose. There are some who interpret Revelation historically, saying it has already been fulfilled, or at least the first eighteen chapters have been fulfilled. Others say it has no meaning at all and there is no reason to study it. However, we believe the pre-millennial, pre-Tribulation Rapture views on eschatology are correct and in accordance with Acts 15:16, that after the Gentile church has been completed and called out of this world, God will once more work through Israel to fulfill His dispensational program (read Romans 11). Misinterpreting the Revelation of John takes the church out of its proper dispensational setting and leads to all kinds of cults, occult groups, false prophets, and a multitude of church divisions claiming the covenant promises to Israel. If ministers and seminaries would properly discern that which God meant for Israel (gospel to the Circumcision) and what God meant for the Gentile church (gospel of the Uncircumcision), there would indeed be fewer denominations and cults. The Apostle Paul claimed that his gospel to the Gentiles, contained in his twelve epistles (with one possible epistle to the Hebrews), was received by revelation from Jesus Christ. The Apocalypse (Revelation) came by revelation of Jesus Christ as explained in the first verse. We also must believe that the gospels, Acts, and the epistles of John, Jude, and Peter were inspired of God. As Christians, saved by faith, we must also accept the providential preservation of all scripture, including the twenty-seven books of the New Testament. Otherwise, every pastor, teacher, and church leader can place their own interpretation as to what to believe or what part to accept. Contemporary scholarship that casts doubt on the Divine Authorship of any scripture is to be scorned as coming from Satan.

We pray that this study on the chronological order of the twenty-seven books of the New Testament will aid the reader in rightly dividing the Word of Truth.

Chapter Sixteen

Is Unity Possible?

"...ye are all the children of God by faith in Christ Jesus...ye are all one in Christ Jesus" (Gal. 3:26,28).

"There is one body, and one Spirit, even as ye are called in one hope of your calling; One Lord, one faith, one baptism, One God and Father of all, who is above all, and through all, and in you all" (Eph. 4:4-6).

"Fulfil ye my joy...being of one accord, of one mind" (Phil. 2:2).

"But unto every one of us is given grace according to the measure of the gift of Christ...Till we all come in the unity of faith...That we henceforth be no more children, tossed to and fro, and carried about with every wind of doctrine, by the sleight of men, and cunning craftiness, whereby they lie in wait to deceive" (Eph. 4:7,13-14).

Paul prayed and worked for the unity of Christians in faith and doctrine. If unity had not been possible, Paul would not have pursued it. Paul did not teach unity through the ecumenical incorporation of all doctrines. He taught that unity was possible through the Gospel that God had given him to preach to the Gentiles.

The Pauline Revelation

"...I certify...that the gospel which was preached of me is not after man. For I neither received it of man, neither was I taught it, but by the revelation of Jesus Christ" (Gal. 1:11-12).

"...the gospel of the uncircumcision was committed unto me, as the gospel of the circumcision was unto Peter" (Gal. 2:7).

"If ye have heard of the dispensation of the grace of God which is given me to you-ward: How that by revelation he made known unto me the mystery...Which in other ages was not made known unto the sons of men..." (Eph. 3:2-3,5).

"...I am made a minister, according to the dispensation of God which is given to me for you, to fulfil the word of God; Even the mystery which hath been hid from ages...To whom God would make known...of this mystery among the Gentiles..." (Col. 1:25-27).

"Now to him that is of power to stablish you according to my gospel, and the preaching of Jesus Christ, according to the revelation of the mystery, which was kept secret since the world began" (Rom. 16:25).

"...a dispensation of the gospel is committed unto me" (1 Cor. 9:17).

"Howbeit for this cause I obtained mercy, that in me first Jesus Christ might shew forth all longsuffering, for a pattern to them which should hereafter believe on him to life everlasting" (1 Tim. 1:16).

The preceding scriptures are just a few of the many in reference to Paul's special dispensational revelation, a message to be preached to the Gentiles for their salvation during a specific period of time. Paul claimed that the revelation of the Gospel to the Gentiles came by special commission from Jesus Christ to himself. He often called it "his" gospel, or "my" gospel, whereby he was called, saved to serve as an example to those who would follow.

According to Paul's Gospel

Salvation

"...The word is nigh thee, even in thy mouth, and in thy heart: that is, the word of faith, which we preach; That if thou shalt confess with thy mouth the Lord Jesus, and shalt believe in thine heart that God hath raised him from the dead, thou shalt be saved" (Rom. 10:8-9).

"For by grace are ye saved through faith; and that not of yourselves: it is the gift of God" (Eph. 2:8).

"I do not frustrate the grace of God: for if righteousness come by the law, then Christ is dead in vain" (Gal. 2:21).

To the Gentiles who knew nothing about the Jew's religion, the Temple, or the law, Paul received from God a message by simple grace: believe in Jesus Christ who died for their sins and be saved. It was not to be a message of salvation that would be contingent on doing anything other than believing and receiving a gift from God. Most denominations have turned Paul's simple message of God's grace into a life-long marathon of trying to refine something that God has already perfected.

Christian Service

"For by grace are ye saved through faith; and that not of yourselves: it is the gift of God: Not of works, lest any man should boast. For we are his workmanship, created in Christ Jesus unto good works, which God hath before ordained that we should walk in them" (Eph. 2:8-10).

"I beseech you therefore, brethren, by the mercies of God, that ye present your bodies a living sacrifice, holy, acceptable unto God, which is your reasonable service" (Rom. 12:1).

"This is a faithful saying, and these things I will that thou affirm constantly, that they which have believed in God might be careful to maintain good works..." (Titus 3:8).

In hundreds of scriptures from the Pauline epistles, the apostle declared that while service and works were not involved in God's grace in offering salvation by faith, good works followed salvation just as a man hired to do work should produce works that were good and acceptable.

Rewards

"Now to him that worketh is the reward not reckoned of grace, but of debt" (Rom. 4:4).

"If any man's work abide which he hath built thereupon, he shall receive a reward. If any man's work shall be burned, he shall suffer loss: but he himself shall be saved; yet so as by fire" (1 Cor. 3:14-15).

"The labourer is worthy of his reward" (1 Tim.5:18).

"For we must all appear before the judgment seat of Christ; that every one may receive the things done in his body, according to that he hath done, whether it be good or bad" (2 Cor. 5:10).

Salvation is not in payment of any debt; it is a gift. Rewards are in settlement of a debt, earned from good works in Christian service.

Communion

"For as often as ye eat this bread, and drink this cup, ye do shew the Lord's death till he come" (1 Cor. 11:26).

According to Paul's instructions, communion is to be observed simply with the bread and the cup, nothing else. It is to be a time of self-examination and remembrance of the atoning death of Jesus Christ for the Christian's salvation. A few churches take communion daily, others weekly, others every three months, and some once a year. Since there is no scriptural rule for the time between taking the Lord's Supper, it does not add or detract from salvation, even if never observed.

Water Baptism

In the Old Testament baptism was a sign of spiritual cleansing from sin, looking forward to Jesus Christ. John the Baptist's baptism was a baptism unto repentance, that is, put off sins of the flesh and get ready for the coming of Messiah as the Kingdom was at hand. Baptism in the early Jerusalem church was a baptism unto remission (decreasing, fading away) after the order of John's baptism as the Kingdom was still being offered.

In the early Gentile churches it appears that water baptism rapidly became a matter of contention and division. Paul wrote to the church at Corinth, *"Is Christ divided? was Paul crucified for you? or were ye baptized in the name of Paul? I thank God that I baptized none of you, but Crispus and Gaius...For Christ sent me not to baptize, but to preach the gospel: not with wisdom of words, lest the cross of Christ should be made of none effect. For the preaching of the cross is to them that perish foolishness; but unto us which are saved it is the power of God"* (1 Cor. 1:13-14,17-18).

According to the gospel committed to Paul to preach to the Gentiles, baptism had no part--nothing at all to do with salvation. But it must have been an issue of contention. Nevertheless, Paul did not definitely forbid water baptism, but cautioned the church about it. Therefore, some church groups like the Quakers and Society of Friends do not practice water baptism. Other denominations like the Church of Christ, Disciples of Christ, and Lutherans believe that baptism is necessary for salvation, or an integral part of the forgiveness of sins which brings salvation. Some Pentecostals believe that water baptism imparts the gifts of the Holy Spirit.

Scriptures

"All scripture is given by inspiration of God, and is profitable for doctrine, for reproof, for correction,

for instruction in righteousness" (2 Tim. 3:16).

Paul's position in reference to the scriptures was that the minds of the writers were dictated to by the Holy Spirit as they wrote. While Paul affirmed that all scripture is profitable to Christians, in 2 Timothy 2:15 he cautioned about "rightly dividing the word of truth." This would mean that while all scriptures are of God and should be studied, his gospel received by revelation was God's personal mail to the Gentile churches.

Ministry of the Holy Spirit

Although Paul referred to himself as the Lord's appointed apostle to the Gentile Christians (and churches), he never referred to what happened to the disciples on the day of Pentecost. While the vast majority of non-Catholic Christendom consider Pentecost of the second chapter of Acts as the beginning of the church, it should seem odd that Paul seems to ignore it. And, it should be kept in mind that the apostle to whom had been given the keys of the Kingdom, the apostle to the Circumcision, Peter, declared this was a miracle prophesied by Joel. Joel prophesied about the Day of the Lord, not the church age. Pentecost of the second chapter of Acts was a sign to Israel that another chance was being given to repent, believe that Jesus Christ was the Messiah, and ask God to send Him back (Acts 3:19-20).

What Did Paul Write to the Churches About the Holy Spirit?

Romans 5:5--The Holy Ghost within Christians helps them to declare the love of God for all men to be saved.

Romans 9:1--The Holy Ghost activates the conscience of Christians to refrain from sinful acts.

Romans 14:17--The Holy Ghost motivates Christians to live joyfully in the Lord.

Romans 15:15--The Holy Ghost fills the Christian with power to be joyful and not to be tempted with doubt.

Romans 15:16--Gentile Christians have been made acceptable to God and sanctified, set apart, by the Holy Ghost.

1 Corinthians 2:13--The Holy Ghost teaches Christians to reconcile the scriptures.

1 Corinthians 3:17--The Christian, while living in the flesh, is the temple of the Holy Ghost (see also 1 Cor. 6:19).

1 Corinthians 12:3--Any person who curses the name of Jesus Christ is not filled with the Holy Ghost (not a Christian). Those who acknowledge Jesus Christ as Lord are led by the Holy Ghost.

1 Corinthians 12:7-10--The Holy Spirit gives talents or abilities: wisdom, knowledge, faith, prophecy, identifying spirits, healing miracles, many tongues (languages), interpreting tongues (languages).

1 Corinthians 12:13--Baptizes the new believer in Jesus Christ into the Lord's body, the church, by a new birth by which he becomes a child of God.

2 Corinthians 6:6--The Holy Spirit motivates patience, kindness, and unselfish love.

2 Corinthians 13:14--The Holy Ghost desires to commune, have fellowship, with each Christian.

Galatians 3:2--The Holy Spirit does not enter into the life of a believer because of any good works, but only responds to the call of faith in Jesus Christ.

Galatians 3:5--Ministers of Jesus Christ are to be filled and led by the Holy Spirit.

Galatians 3:14--The promise of the Holy Spirit (joy, security, eternal life, resurrection) is claimed by faith rather than works.

Galatians 4:6-9--The Holy Spirit testifies to Christians that they are sons of God and heirs of Jesus Christ.

Galatians 5:5--Righteousness of Jesus Christ is imputed by faith, and then, the Holy Spirit helps the Christian to walk upright before the world.

Galatians 5:16--The only way to overcome the lusts of the flesh is to live in the Holy Spirit.

Galatians 5:17--The Holy Spirit attacks the lusts of the flesh, and the flesh attacks the Holy Spirit.

Galatians 5:18--If the Christian allows the Holy Spirit to lead him, then he depends upon Jesus Christ for strength rather than depending upon himself.

Galatians 5:22--The fruit of the Holy Spirit in the Christian's life is love, joy, and peace.

Galatians 5:25--Because Christians are born again by the Holy Spirit they should live each day in the leading of the Holy Spirit.

Galatians 6:8--A life planted in the lusts of the flesh will reap corruption, but a life planted in the Holy Spirit will reap everlasting life.

Ephesians 1:13--The Holy Spirit seals the salvation of the Christian until the resurrection of the body.

Ephesians 1:14--The Holy Spirit is the earnest, or just a small down payment, of the Christian's inheritance in Jesus Christ.

Ephesians 1:18--It is through the ministry of the Holy Spirit that Gentiles who were without any hope were given access to God.

Ephesians 3:5--The Holy Spirit reveals to ministers the message of the gospel of grace.

Ephesians 3:16--The Holy Spirit gives power to the inner man to remain strong in the faith of Jesus

Christ.

Ephesians 4:3--The Holy Spirit ministers to bring peace and unity among all Christians.

Ephesians 4:4--There is only one Holy Spirit, one with God in the Trinity.

Ephesians 4:30--Christians are not to grieve the Holy Spirit by sinful deeds, because the Holy Spirit keeps the Christians saved by His power.

Ephesians 6:17--The sword or weapon of the Holy Spirit against the Devil is the Word of God.

Ephesians 6:18--Christians are to pray as the Holy Spirit leads them to ask of God.

Philippians 2:1--Fellowship with the Holy Spirit is to be desired.

Colossians 1:8--The will of the Holy Spirit for is Christians to love one another.

1 Thessalonians 1:5--The Holy Ghost gives boldness to preach the Gospel.

1 Thessalonians 1:6--The Holy Ghost gives courage to the lost to believe the Gospel even under persecution.

1 Thessalonians 4:8--Those who reject the Gospel reject the Holy Spirit.

1 Thessalonians 5:19--Christians are exhorted to not quench, or try to cut off, the filling and leading of the Holy Spirit.

2 Thessalonians 2:13--Christians are sanctified (set apart for God) by the Holy Spirit.

1 Timothy 3:16--The raising of Jesus Christ from the dead by the power of the Holy Spirit is part of the mystery of the incarnation.

1 Timothy 4:1--The Holy Spirit speaks forthrightly and plainly to Christians in the last days concerning evil spirits and false teachers.

2 Timothy 1:14--The Holy Ghost helps Christians to remember those things which are good and forget those things which are unprofitable.

Titus 3:5--The Holy Ghost renews the man who is dead in sin to new life in Jesus Christ.

Romans 8:1--The Christians who seek the leading of the Holy Spirit rather than seeking after the satisfaction of the flesh will not come under condemnation before the world.

Romans 8:11--The Holy Spirit raised the body of Jesus Christ from the dead to eternal and immortal life. Just so, the Holy Spirit will raise the bodies of those who have died in the faith of Jesus Christ to eternal and immortal life.

Romans 8:15--The Holy Spirit testifies to the spirits of Christians that they are the children of God.

Romans 8:26--When Christians do not know how to pray or what to pray for, the Holy Spirit prays for them.

The lengthy, preceding roster of scriptures should indicate to the reader the importance of the ministry of the Holy Spirit within the gospel of grace that Paul received to preach to the Gentiles. While these scriptures on the Holy Spirit do not contain every reference to the subject, they do make up the majority. Omitted in this list are references to the Holy Spirit in Hebrews. While I believe that Paul did write Hebrews, it was written to the Jewish church in Jerusalem and not entirely relevant to this particular part of our study.

From these scriptures we can easily determine that the most important mission of the Holy Spirit, as explained by Paul, to the church is:

1. by the new birth create a new creature in Christ Jesus by faith;
2. give power to the new Christian to proclaim the

Gospel and witness to others;
3. seal the salvation of the Christian until the day of redemption;
4. bring peace, joy, and continuing faith to the Christians;
5. fill, lead, guide, and teach the Christian;
6. impart talents to the Christian that will glorify God; and
7. raise the bodies of Christians to immortal and eternal life at the resurrection (Rapture).

Most of the individual missions of the Holy Spirit to the church, and Christians, are stressed over and over. However, the gift of tongues is mentioned only twice in his first epistle to the church at Corinth, which was a worldly, confused church. Miracles are mentioned in the twelfth chapter of 1 Corinthians and again in the third chapter of Galatians. The Galatian churches are also spiritually confused and misled. Healing, as a gift of the Holy Spirit, is mentioned one time in the twelfth chapter of 1 Corinthians.

The reason for this fact being mentioned is that in these last days new doctrines have originated on these three lesser gifts of the Holy Spirit that have further divided Christendom, creating a multitude of new churches.

In the Old Testament it is prophesied that when the Messiah came He would heal the sick, make the lame to walk, the blind to see, cast out devils, raise the dead, and do many other wonderful miracles. Every miracle that Jesus Christ did was in some way a fulfillment of an Old Testament prophecy to prove to Israel that He was indeed the Messiah. There is no evidence that Jesus Christ spoke in any other language than that which was common in Israel at the time--Hebrew and/

or Aramaic. Up until Acts 28:28, Paul was commissioned to declare to the Jews (first) that the Messiah had come, and to the Gentiles that God had favored them with a Savior. Healings and miracles were signs to the Jews. Also, on the day of Pentecost the fact that the disciples were speaking quite fluently some seventeen or eighteen languages to the Jews who had returned from other nations was also a sign that God was ready to pour out His Spirit upon the entire nation (Zech. 12:10). When Peter went to see Cornelius, and preached the Word concerning the birth, death, and resurrection of Jesus Christ, this Gentile spoke in tongues and the Jews with Peter were astonished. However, this was received as a sign by the Jews that God had granted to the Gentiles "repentance unto life" in accordance with the gospel of the Kingdom that Peter preached.

The main signs to the Jews that continued up until the destruction of the Temple and the termination of the nation of Judah were healings, miracles, and tongues (as speaking in other languages). Throughout the book of Acts, and particularly the last chapter of Acts, it is declared that as a race of people the Jews would not believe, but that the Gentiles would believe. In Isaiah 28:11-12, it was prophesied that men with other tongues would speak to Israel, but Israel would still not believe. Paul stated in 1 Corinthians 14:21-22, *"In the law it is written, With men of other tongues and other lips will I speak unto this people; and yet for all that will they not hear me, saith the Lord. Wherefore tongues are for a sign, not to them that believe* [Gentile Christians], *but to them that believe not* [Jews]...." Not only were the early Gentile Christians in some cases given the gift of tongues as a sign to Israel, but also miracles and healings were likewise signs to the Jews. This truth cannot be intelligently disputed. After Israel ceased to be a nation, there was no longer a need for these signs. Paul indicated in the thirteenth chapter of 1 Corinthians, verse eight, that the gifts of tongues would cease. I have led Christian mission tours in many foreign countries. On almost every tour there have been Catholics, Baptists, Pentecostals, Charismatics, etc. But I have yet to see any tour member who never studied a foreign language go up to a Russian, Chinaman, Arab, etc., and speak to that foreigner in his own language. Many do claim to speak in "unknown" tongues, but the word "unknown" in the King James text is in italics, indicating it was inserted by the translators. Paul said that no person in church should speak in a tongue or language not known to the congregation without an interpreter. Paul's advice certainly makes good sense. This gift of the Holy Spirit in the early church has been misinterpreted by so many today that it is absolutely ridiculous.

Recently I was in a regional meeting of the National Religious Broadcasters in Dallas, Texas. In one of the sessions a prominent television evangelist spoke, and in the course of his message reference was made to the number of people he had raised from the dead the past month. Of course, those who claim all the Holy Ghost gifts present in the early church should be able to raise the dead in order to be completely biblical. But when I asked this evangelist for the names, death certificates, and obituary notices of those he had raised from the dead, he became highly indignant.

Does God still heal the sick? Yes, when it is for His glory. Can the Holy Ghost still empower Christians to speak in other languages? Yes, but I personally know of no incident where it is presently occurring. To misappropriate the early Pentecostal signs to Israel has, I believe, further divided Christians and caused unnecessary confusion.

Eschatology

As already referred to repeatedly, the first century church expected Jesus Christ to return in their lifetime. As long as Israel was a nation and the Temple was standing, this expectation was indeed a valid possibility. Jesus said in Matthew 23:38-39, *"Behold, your house is left unto you desolate. For I say unto you, Ye shall not see me henceforth, till ye shall say, Blessed is he that cometh in the name of the Lord."* Beyond the destruction of the Temple in A.D. 70, Jesus Himself said that His return depended upon the nation of Israel coming to the acceptance of the truth that He is the Messiah. Nevertheless, Peter, John, and the early Christian disciples in Israel worked to bring about this promise when Jesus Himself indicated it would not occur until much later. Paul himself looked for the return of Jesus Christ and even returned to Israel, although warned against returning three times by the Holy Spirit, to help bring about repentance and conversion.

Before considering contemporary eschatological views of the churches, let us again appraise the prophetic setting of the dispensation of grace in relation to God's eternal plan and purpose. This was the main purpose of Paul's request for a conference with the Jerusalem church in A.D. 50.

1. *"And after they had held their peace, James answered, saying, Men and brethren, hearken unto me: Simeon hath declared how God at the first did visit the Gentiles, to take out of them a people for his name"* (Acts 15:13-14). Although some relate Peter's statement to the call of Abraham, it seems evident that the apostle was referring to a contemporary event, the beginning of the Gentile church age. Peter also, at least at this time, still

separated the all-Jewish church in Israel under covenant promises from the Gentiles being converted
through the preaching of Paul.

2. *"And to this agree the words of the prophets; as it is written"*
(Acts 15:15). Although the prophets knew nothing
about God calling out of the Gentiles a people for the
Lord's Name, there is nothing written by the prophets that contradicts the church age.

3. *"After this I will return, and will build again the tabernacle
of David, which is fallen down; and I will build again the
ruins thereof, and I will set it up"* (Acts 15:16). After God
is finished taking out of the world a people from the
Gentiles for His Name, Jesus Christ will return and
build again the Temple and restore God's covenant
with Israel. Therefore, this church age, the dispensation of God's grace, will end. God will stop taking out
of the world Gentiles saved by the Gospel preached
by Paul, the apostle to the Gentiles. It seems obvious
from 1 Thessalonians 4:13-18 that this is when the
resurrection and translation of the church will occur
even those Christians alive will be changed and meet
the Lord in the air. After this, according to the fifth
chapter of 1 Thessalonians, the Lord will return and
there will be a time of God's wrath (the Day of the
Lord, the Great Tribulation) upon the earth. According to the chronology of James' and Peter's declaration in the fifteenth chapter of Acts, Jesus will return
and restore the Temple and the Jewish nation. Why?

4. *"That the residue of men might seek after the Lord, and all
the Gentiles, upon whom my name is called, saith the Lord,
who doeth all these things"* (Acts 15:17). It is likewise
evident that this verse refers to the Millennium which
will come after the Great Tribulation. But before
Jesus returns to bring in the Kingdom age, according
to the tenth chapter of Romans, the Jews who have

made it through this time of Jacob's Trouble will come to the knowledge that Jesus Christ is both Messiah and Savior; they will cry out for God to send Him back; they will be saved by believing that He died for their sins.

The changing views of the early church regarding the second coming of Jesus Christ is referred to by Edward Gibbons on page 187 of *The Decline and Fall of the Roman Empire*:

"In the primitive church the influence of truth was very powerfully strengthened by an opinion which, however it may deserve respect for its usefulness and antiquity, has not been found agreeable to experience. It was universally believed that the end of the world, and the kingdom of heaven, were at hand. The near approach of this wonderful event had been predicted by the apostles; the tradition of it was preserved by their earliest disciples, and those who understood in their literal sense the discourses of Christ himself were obligated to expect the second and glorious coming of the Son of Man in the clouds, before that generation was totally extinguished which had beheld his humble condition upon earth, and which might still be witness of the calamities of the Jews under Vespasian or Hadrian. The revolution of seventeen centuries has instructed us not to press too closely the mysterious language of prophecy and revelation; but as long as, for wise purposes, this error was permitted to subsist in the church, it was productive of the most salutary effects on the faith and practice of Christians, who lived in the awful expectation of that moment when the globe itself, and all the various races of mankind, should tremble at

the appearance of their divine Judge.

"The ancient and popular doctrine of the Millennium was intimately connected with the second coming of Christ. As the works of the creation had been finished in six days, their duration in their present state, according to a tradition which was attributed to the prophet Elijah, was fixed to six thousand years. By the same analogy it was inferred that this long period of labour and contention, which was now almost elapsed, would be succeeded by a joyful Sabbath of a thousand years; and that Christ, with their triumphant band of the saints and the elect who had escaped death, or who had been miraculously revived, would reign upon the earth till the time appointed for the last and general resurrection. Pleasing was this hope to the mind of believers."

Gibbons verifies that the primitive church expected Jesus Christ to come back in their lifetime, but after the destruction of the Temple brought about by Vespasian and the dispersion by Hadrian, the church then looked forward to Christ's return in A.D. 2000. Gibbons continues on this subject to say that before this glorious Sabbath with its New Jerusalem comes on the earth, that Mystery Babylon, or what was interpreted to be Rome, must be destroyed. Thus, the early church believed in the pre-millennial return of Jesus Christ as the prophetic Word declares. In the contemporary church of today Christendom is divided into three main divisions regarding eschatological beliefs: pre-millennial--those who believe that Jesus Christ will return after the Great Tribulation to bring in the Kingdom; post-millennial--those who believe that the church will first bring in the Kingdom and then Jesus will come back and take charge; A-millennial--those who believe that the Millennium has already occurred, is occurring now, or there will never be a Millennium. Also, regarding the end of the church age, some believe as we do that the translation of the church (Rapture) will occur prior to the Great Tribulation; others believe it will occur at the midway point of the Great Tribulation; and still others believe Christians will go through the entire seven years of the Great Tribulation. These different prophetic positions are referred to as pre-Trib, mid-Trib, and post-Trib.

The reasons for these different views on biblical eschatology, which have further divided Christendom into many divisions, is that theologians have failed to discern the difference in God's plan and purpose for Israel with that of God's plan and purpose for the church of the dispensation of grace. If all Christians would consider and study the epistles of Paul, to whom was given the message for the Gentile church, there would be no reason for differences of opinion on this subject.

The Sabbath or Sunday

"Thus the heavens and the earth were finished, and all the host of them. And on the seventh day God ended his work which he had made; and he rested on the seventh day from all his work which he had made. And God blessed the seventh day, and sanctified it: because that in it he had rested from all his work which God created and made" (Gen. 2:1-3).

"Remember the sabbath day, to keep it holy. Six days shalt thou labour, and do all thy work: But the seventh day is the sabbath of the Lord thy God...For in six days the Lord made heaven and

earth...wherefore the Lord blessed the sabbath day, and hallowed it" (Exod. 20:8-11).

"And the Lord spake unto Moses, saying, Speak thou also unto the children of Israel, saying, Verily my sabbaths ye shall keep: for it is a sign between me and you throughout your generations...every one that defileth it shall surely be put to death..." (Exod. 31:12-14).

"And it came to pass, that he went through the corn fields on the sabbath day; and his disciples began, as they went, to pluck the ears of corn. And the Pharisees said unto him, Behold, why do they on the sabbath day that which is not lawful?...And he said unto them, The sabbath was made for man, and not man for the sabbath" (Mark 2:23-24,27).

"And upon the first day of the week, when the disciples came together to break bread, Paul preached unto them, ready to depart on the morrow; and continued his speech until midnight" (Acts 20:7).

"Now concerning the collection for the saints, as I have given order to the churches of Galatia, even so do ye. Upon the first day of the week let every one of you lay by him in store, as God hath prospered him, that there be no gatherings when I come" (1 Cor. 16:1-2).

"Let us hold fast the profession of our faith without wavering...And let us consider one another to provoke unto love and to good works: Not forsaking the assembling of ourselves together, as the manner of some is; but exhorting one another: and so much the

more, as ye see the day approaching" (Heb. 10:23-25).

"What advantage then hath the Jew? or what profit is there of circumcision? Much every way: chiefly, because that unto them were committed the oracles of God" (Rom. 3:1-2).

Saturday is the Sabbath. It always has been and always will be. Even before the law was given to Moses, it is apparent that Israelites had kept the Sabbath. God commanded in the law to Israel, "Remember the Sabbath..." indicating that they had observed it previously. The Sabbath has always been a sign to Israel of the Kingdom age, the seventh millennium, when the covenant promises will be fulfilled. The epistle of Hebrews was written to the disciples of the church at Jerusalem. In this epistle there are eleven references to the Sabbath being the promised Millennium. In the fourth chapter of Hebrews we read that Jesus would have brought in that day of rest, meaning the Sabbath, if Israel had believed. No such references to the Sabbath are found in the epistles to the Gentile churches.

There is no evidence that the Gentile ever kept the Sabbath according to the law. Jesus was constantly challenged over keeping the Sabbath because He had come to fulfill the law, and He was the Lord of the Sabbath. The Jerusalem church evidently continued to keep the Sabbath. The Gentile churches never kept the Sabbath, nor were they ever commanded to do so. The destination of the church of the dispensation of grace is heavenly, while the destination of saved Israel is earthly. From what information we have in the epistles of Paul, it seems that the Gentile churches met on the first day of the week for worship and fellowship. The Seventh-

Day Adventists claim that the Roman Catholic Church changed the Sabbath to Sunday, but in the Epistle of Barnabas credited to the first century, Dionysius of Corinth in A.D. 170 and Clemens Alex in A.D. 194, all make mention of the Gentile Christians meeting for assembly and worship on the first day of the week, the day of the Lord's resurrection. So Gentile Christians meeting for worship on Sunday was the custom two hundred years or more before Constantine established the Catholic Church. Paul wrote to the Gentile Christians in Colossians 2:16, *"Let no man therefore judge you in meat, or in drink, or in respect of an holyday, or of the new moon, or of the sabbath days."*

The preceding should be more than sufficient evidence that the Seventh-Day Adventist Church is in error in contending that all churches must observe the Sabbath. While the custom established in the first century churches indicates that the Gentile Christians met on Sunday, there is no such direct commandment or ordinance. According to the Scriptures, Christians can assemble for worship, fellowship, and evangelism on any day of the week or year they so choose, and as often as they may decide. But again, this is just another misinterpretation of Scripture that has resulted in church divisions.

Tithes

Tithes and offerings for the Lord's work is another matter of contention among churches that often split congregations into various factions. While Cain and Abel gave offerings to the Lord, the first place in Scripture where the tithe is mentioned is when Abraham gave his tithe to Melchizedek. Under the law, the Israelites were commanded to give tithes of everything to the storehouse, which was under the supervision of the priests. The tithe included all animals, vegetables, grain, fruit, and money. Ancient records indicate that most of the time, tithes were given voluntarily, and only on occasions were they taken by force. The Scriptures indicate, for example in 2 Chronicles 31:10, that when the Israelites were faithful in the matter of tithing God blessed them and the nation. When they withheld their tithes, God was displeased. This was the message of the prophet Malachi: *"Will a man rob God? Yet ye have robbed me. But ye say, Wherein have we robbed thee? In tithes and offerings. Ye are cursed with a curse: for ye have robbed me, even this whole nation. Bring ye all the tithes into the storehouse, that there may be meat in mine house, and prove me now herewith, saith the Lord of hosts, if I will not open you the windows of heaven, and pour you out a blessing, that there shall not be room enough to receive it"* (Mal. 3:8-10). This is a favorite scripture of many pastors in making the annual church-tithe drive. But this scripture is not for the church, because Gentile Christians were never commanded or exhorted to tithe . It is also difficult to tie the local church to the storehouse of the Old Testament.

Tithing is mentioned three times in the gospels-- Matthew 23:23, Luke 11:42, and Luke 18:12. In all three scriptures, tithing refers to the self-righteous acts of the Pharisees. Tithing is also mentioned four times in the seventh chapter of Hebrews, but here it also refers back to tithing by Abraham and Levi. If tithing to the storehouse is as important as most churches stress, then surely it would have been mentioned at least once in the epistles to the Gentile churches. But the Gentiles were never asked to tithe. To take tithes to build huge churches where the Name of Jesus Christ is blasphemed is an abomination.

Christian giving is mentioned in several scriptures.

As we have already referred to, in 1 Corinthians 16:1-3 the church members at Corinth were encouraged to give liberally for the needs of the saints at Jerusalem. As it is today in Israel, it is difficult for those who name the Name of Jesus Christ to find jobs, so the disciples needed outside assistance. Paul wrote again to the church at Corinth, *"But this I say, He which soweth sparingly shall reap also sparingly; and he which soweth bountifully shall reap also bountifully. Every man according as he purposeth in his heart, so let him give; not grudgingly, or of necessity: for God loveth a cheerful giver"* (2 Cor. 9:6-7).

What few instructions we have by Paul for the Gentiles supporting the local church or foreign missions stipulate:

1. Give with a willing and cheerful attitude; not just because of pressure or an emergency.
2. The Christian should make up his or her mind that giving to the Lord's work is the right thing to do.
3. Those who give generously will be rewarded generously by the Lord.
4. Give in proportion as God has blessed.
5. Give regularly in accordance to a pre-determined schedule.
6. Under the law, one-tenth belonged to God. Under grace, everything belongs to God.

I have heard Christians testify in church how God has blessed them since they determined to tithe their income. Did God bless them because they tithed? Or did God bless them because they gave as He had prospered them and with a willing and cheerful heart? Probably, the latter would be the real truth. Although tithing is not directed to Gentile Christians in the New Testament, it is reasonable to assume if the Jews tithed under the law, we can do no less under grace. Even Paul wrote to the Christians at Corinth that the more they gave, the more God would bless them.

Some churches stress storehouse tithing; others do not. And although the manner and method of giving may not be a major doctrine, it is a matter of individual conscience and it has caused divisions among Christians and churches alike.

There are many other items of conscience, doctrine, and liturgy which have contributed to the establishing and/or splitting of churches and denominations even further. However, in this chapter we have attempted to analyze only the major factors.

Chapter Seventeen

Rapture and Resurrection

In studying the messages of Peter and the disciples of the Jerusalem church to Israel, as given in the first eight chapters of Acts, we find little or nothing about the resurrection of believers who die in the faith. But as the Jerusalem church preached the gospel of the Kingdom, this is not surprising. Resurrection was no mystery to national Israel under the promises of the covenants, and Peter preached to Israel the return of Jesus Christ to bring in the "times of refreshing" (the fulfillment of covenant promises). Had resurrection been an integral part of Peter's gospel to the Circumcision, we would have more confusion in the churches today than we already have. But even so, on the subject of resurrection we find a multitude of doctrines and beliefs. It seems that each denomination or sect has its own particular and peculiar views as to how Christians will be raised, when they will be raised, what they will be raised to, and what will follow resurrection. This mass confusion is not confined to modern churches; there was confusion about resurrection in Paul's day in the assembly at Corinth and also in the church at Thessalonica. This consternation about resurrection among Gentile believers has come about because they have attempted to relate or associate their hope in Christ with the promises made by God to Israel in the covenants.

Resurrection was a definite promise for those Israelites who kept the commandments because the law pointed forward to the Messiah who would raise the righteous dead, according to the law, when He would bring in the Kingdom. When Jesus was talking with Martha about the death of Lazarus, she replied, *"...I know that he shall rise again in the resurrection of the last day* [meaning the Day of the Lord]" (John 11:24). There was no need for Peter to preach on resurrection, for in the gospel of the Kingdom which he preached all Israel was fully informed on the subject.

Israel's order of resurrection was established by many of the Old Testament prophets, but we will discuss just one account, recorded in Isaiah 26:16-18, *"Lord, in trouble have they visited thee, they poured out a prayer when thy chastening was upon them. Like as a woman with child, that draweth near the time of her delivery, is in pain, and crieth out in her pangs; so have we been in thy sight, O Lord. We have been with child, we have been in pain, we have as it were brought forth wind; we have not wrought any deliverance in the earth; neither have the inhabitants of the world fallen."*

In the preceding verses, the prophet had been referring to Israel's dispersion in the nations, and the reigning of other lords over them. As the prophetic scene turned to the refounding of Israel as a nation, the national estate of Israel continued to remain perplexing and frustrating. The enemies of Israel still stand; Israel remains impotent to be a blessing to the nations of the world as promised in the covenants, and she stands as a woman with child, knowing that the time of her deliverance is near, yet helpless to defend herself against those who would destroy both her and her child. This prophecy corresponds to the twelfth chapter of Revelation, but we must remember that Jesus Christ as the man-child is presented from a covenant position as the King to be brought forth by Israel to rule all nations.

This is why so many have trouble understanding the "woman" of Revelation 12.

Remember, this is a Tribulation setting, as we read in Isaiah 26:19-21: *"Thy dead men shall live, together with my dead body shall they arise. Awake and sing, ye that dwell in dust; for thy dew is as the dew of herbs, and the earth shall cast out the dead. Come, my people, enter thou into thy chambers, and shut thy doors about thee: hide thyself as it were for a little moment, until the indignation be overpast. For, behold, the Lord cometh out of his place to punish the inhabitants of the earth for their iniquity...."*

The resurrection of the saints of Israel is to occur after the Lord has punished the inhabitants of the earth for their iniquity when He comes again, signifying Armageddon. After the indignation is past and Israel comes out of the chamber (returns to the land), then the Lord will raise the saints who have died.

We have this same picture given to us of the resurrection of the saints in Daniel 12:1-2: *"And at that time* [meaning the rise of Antichrist] *shall Michael stand up, the great prince which standeth for the children of thy people* [Israel]: *and there shall be a time of trouble, such as never was since there was a nation even to that same time: and at that time thy people shall be delivered, every one that shall be found written in the book. And many of them that sleep in the dust of the earth shall awake, some to everlasting life, and some to shame and everlasting contempt."*

All scripture relating to the resurrection of the saints of Israel indicates that their resurrection is to occur after the Tribulation at the coming of the Lord to bring in the Kingdom. It is, of course, understood from the twentieth chapter of Revelation that the lost dead of all ages are to be raised at one time at the Great White Throne judgment. It is well for us to remember that nothing is said about the saints of Israel rising to meet the Lord in the air and nothing is promised in the nature of a physical change to those Israelites living at the coming of the Lord. The promise to living Israel at that time is that the Holy Spirit will be poured out upon them and they shall be called the sons of God.

We note in Matthew 27:52-53 that after the resurrection of Jesus, many bodies of the saints of Israel arose and appeared to many in Jerusalem. I think it is important to stress here that these were *bodies* of the saints and this was another Kingdom sign to Israel. The fact that the bodies of these saints which arose went into Jerusalem is also significant, indicating the manner of Israel's resurrection.

While there are scriptures in Genesis, Job, and some other books of the Old Testament relating to resurrection outside of Israel, the prophets of Israel did not speak of a resurrection for the Gentiles. After the law came, the hope of resurrection for the Gentiles lay in becoming Jewish proselytes.

It is understandable therefore, as to why the members of the church at Corinth became concerned over the matter of the resurrection of those who had by faith received the gospel which Paul preached. Having no volume of scripture concerning the resurrection of the church, we read in 1 Corinthians 15:12 that many believed there was no resurrection for Christians. They may have believed in a spirit life hereafter, but they discounted the possibility of a tangible bodily life after the manner of which was promised to the saints of Israel. Paul wrote the Corinthian church concerning the resurrection of those who are in Christ, meaning of course, those that are added to the body of Christ by faith. Paul speaks to them not about the resurrection of Israel, but about their resurrection. *"But if there be no resurrection of the dead, then is Christ not risen...And if Christ be not raised, your faith is vain; ye are yet in your sins. Then they also which are fallen asleep in Christ are perished...But now is Christ risen from the dead, and become the firstfruits of them that slept"* (1 Cor. 15:13,17-18,20). Paul is speaking of the resurrection of those "in Christ," those added to the body of Christ, and if the Head of the body, who is Christ, has risen, He will also raise the *body*.

Paul continued this teaching in verses twenty-two and twenty-three: *"For as in Adam all die, even so in Christ shall all be made alive. But every man in his own order: Christ the firstfruits; afterward they that are Christ's at his coming."* The timetable for all resurrection of the righteous is at the second coming of Christ, but Paul here refers to something entirely new--every man raised in his own order. The word in the original text for order is *tagma*, meaning "rank" or "company," as in a long parade of soldiers passing in review. Paul taught the Christians at Corinth they would be raised according to their own order. Where did Paul get this new teaching? He reveals the source in 1 Corinthians 15:51-52: *"Behold, I shew you a mystery; We shall not all sleep, but we shall all be changed, In a moment, in the twinkling of an eye, at the last trump: for the trumpet shall sound, and the dead shall be raised incorruptible, and we shall be changed."*

Paul said, "I shew you a mystery." The truth concerning the resurrection of the church was received by Paul from Christ by direct revelation. It was a part of that mystery, not revealed to any man of any former age until it was given to Paul. When some say, "Well, it's a mystery to me where you get the Rapture of the church in the Bible," they don't realize how close they have come to finding the answer for themselves. The resurrection of the members of the body of Christ, to which the saved of this dispensation belong, will not be a resurrection to an earthly kingdom, but rather it will be a celestial body to reign in heavenly places with the Lord Jesus Christ.

Paul disclosed more of the revelation concerning the mystery of the Rapture of the church in 1 Thessalonians 4:13-18: *"But I would not have you to be ignorant, brethren, concerning them which are asleep, that ye sorrow not, even as others which have no hope. For if we believe that Jesus died and rose again, even so them also which sleep in Jesus will God bring with him. For this we say unto you by the word of the Lord, that we which are alive and remain unto the coming of the Lord shall not prevent them which are asleep. For the Lord himself shall descend from heaven with a shout, with the voice of the archangel, and with the trump of God: and the dead in Christ shall rise first: Then we which are alive and remain shall be caught up together with them in the clouds, to meet the Lord in the air: and so shall we ever be with the Lord. Wherefore comfort one another with these words."*

The resurrection of the Gentile church, or the body of Christ, will be different from that of Israel in that it will occur suddenly--"in the twinkling of an eye"-- evidently secret from the world. The dead in Christ will be resurrected first, immediately followed by Christians yet alive when this glorious event takes place. The fact that the Christians who are alive will need a bodily transformation is obvious, and Paul wrote to the Corinthians that all would be changed.

As to the time of this separate resurrection of the church, Paul gives this added insight in 1 Thessalonians 5:1-5: *"But of the times and the seasons, brethren, ye have no need that I write unto you. For yourselves know perfectly that the day of the Lord so cometh as a thief in the night. For when they shall say, Peace and safety; then sudden destruction cometh upon them, as travail upon a woman with child; and they shall not escape. But ye, brethren, are not in darkness, that that day should overtake you as a thief. Ye are all the children of the light, and the children of the day: we are not of the night, nor of darkness."*

Paul informed the Christians at Thessalonica that he had no need to write to them of signs relating to the times and seasons of the second coming of Christ because they would know when the Rapture of the church was near. From the fulfilling of the Old Testament prophecies given by our Lord Jesus Christ concerning the end of the age, Christians will know their date to meet the Lord in the air is near. He refers to the coming of the Day of the Lord upon the world as a thief in the night, but then Paul said that "ye," meaning those in Christ, are not of this night, but of the day.

The prophecies concerning the resurrection of Israel state emphatically that living Israel must first go through a great time of trouble before the saints that sleep would arise. But there is no such indication that the church will go through the Tribulation. We find evidences of living Israel all through the Tribulation, as described in Revelation, but no evidence whatever of the church.

Paul wrote concerning the gathering of the church unto Christ in the second chapter of Thessalonians that there would first be a falling away, and then he indicates that the Holy Spirit would be taken out of the world so that the Antichrist could be revealed to the world. If the bodies of the members of the Lord's church are "temples of the Holy Spirit," and if, according to the mystery, our salvation is sealed by the Holy Spirit unto the day of redemption, then how can the Holy Spirit be taken out of the world without also removing the church from the world at the same time? That order for the resurrection of the church, which we refer to as the Rapture of the church, must be scheduled to take place before the Tribulation. That body of truth which Jesus Christ gave to Paul to preach to the Gentiles envisions no obligation of the church to go through the Tribulation.

Many wonder why Christians cannot agree on even the most paramount of all doctrines: the resurrection of the body. Some believe the soul sleeps until the resurrection; some believe the soul goes at death to be with the Lord to await resurrection; others believe the dead of all ages, both saved and unsaved, will be raised at one time; and still others believe (like the Sadducees) that there will be no resurrection. The subject of resurrection has helped to further divide Christendom into splits and divisions because of differences in scriptural interpretation.

In the Old Testament Israel is warned to expect the "time of Jacob's Trouble" before their deliverance. In Daniel alone Israel is warned three times to expect first the Abomination of Desolation. Jesus warned the Jews about the Abomination of Desolation in the Olivet Discourse. If the church is to go through the Tribulation, would we not expect also to be warned? Paul said of that day, "...*sudden destruction cometh upon them* [the unsaved world]...*For God hath not appointed us to wrath...*" (1 Thess. 5:3,9).

Paul writes of the time of Great Tribulation spoken of in Matthew 24:21-22 by Jesus: "*For yourselves know perfect that the day of the Lord so cometh as a thief in the night. For when they shall say, Peace and safety; then sudden destruction cometh upon them, as travail upon a woman with child; and they shall not escape*" (1 Thess. 5:2-3). The unsaved will not escape destruction in the Great Tribulation, indicating the saved will "escape" destruction. How? Paul has just explained the way of escape in the concluding verses of the preceding chapter: "*Then we which are alive and remain shall be caught up together with them in the clouds, to meet the Lord in the air...*" (1 Thess. 4:17).

I point out again that we hold no illusions that this book will either promote or aid any kind of ecumenical movement within Christendom. I do pray that this study will help you as an individual Christian understand why some churches believe one way and still others believe another way. I say again that the reason there are so many churches is because of a common failure to rightly divide the Word of God as recorded in the first fifteen chapters of the book of Acts. May God bless each one who profits from this study, and may we all be more charitable one toward another,

> *"Till we all come in the unity of the faith, and the knowledge of the Son of God, unto a perfect man, unto the measure of the stature of the fulness of Christ: That we henceforth be no more children, tossed to and fro, and carried about with every wind of doctrine, by the sleight of men, and cunning craftiness, whereby they lie in wait to deceive; But speaking the truth in love, may grow up into him in all things, which is the head, even Christ"* (Eph. 4:13-15).